CELEBRATING HOLY DAYS

& FEAST DAYS YEAR ROUND

Celebrating Holy Days & Feast Days Year Round

Over 150 Faith-Filled Activities and Prayers for Kids

Patricia Mathson

TWENTY-THIRD PUBLICATIONS
twentythirdpublications.com

TWENTY-THIRD PUBLICATIONS
977 Hartford Turnpike Unit A
Waterford, CT 06385
(860) 437-3012 or (800) 321-0411
www.twentythirdpublications.com

Cover photo / Image credits: stock.adobe.com

ISBN: 978-1-62785-749-9
Printed in the U.S.A.

bayard A division of Bayard, Inc.

Contents

INTRODUCTION

The ideas in this book help busy catechists, teachers, and families explore twenty-five special days with children throughout the church year. This encourages children to make the connection between their lives, their God, their church, and their world. Walking through the year together lets children experience God's love for them and shows them ways to share that love with other people.

Celebrating special days—including new ones such as World Day of Prayer for the Care of Creation, Sunday of the Word of God, and Mary, Mother of the Church—with child-friendly activities is important. We must help children connect their lives to the Sunday liturgy beyond the classroom.

This book is a one-stop resource. There are more than 150 child-friendly ideas and activities to engage children in learning so they can live their faith in God. These include action prayers, small-group projects, service ideas, posters, echo pantomimes, crafts, sharing questions, community-building activities, and many others. The activities encourage children to live as disciples of Jesus Christ.

Ideas in this book invite children ages 5 to 11 to follow Jesus Christ throughout the year. The ideas are easily adapted for other ages or abilities. Choose the activities for each day that fit the interests and abilities of your group of children. A calendar of dates for the current year is always found on the website for the United States Conference of Catholic Bishops (usccb.org) under "Events."

These activities do not need to be done with children on the exact day being celebrated. Children can participate in activities ahead of time to prepare them for the special day or afterward as a reminder to live the meaning of the day in their lives. Special days have an impact beyond the day itself. The values should echo through our lives.

It is important for children to learn that God calls each of us to make a difference in the lives of others. Everyone can do something. Celebrating special days helps children and all of us have hope in God, hope in one another, and hope in the future.

World Day of Prayer for the Care of Creation

POPE FRANCIS CHOSE SEPTEMBER 1 AS A DAY TO REMEMBER THAT GOD CALLS US TO TAKE CARE OF CREATION. The beauty of creation shows us how much our God loves us now and forever. In *Laudato Si': On Care for Our Common Home* (vatican.va), Pope Francis says, "The world is a gift which we have freely received and must share with others." On this World Day of Prayer for the Care of Creation, we remember that God created our world to be shared by all people. Caring for creation also means caring for one another.

Patron saint of ecology

World Day of Prayer for the Care of Creation is a good time to share with children the story of St. Francis of Assisi, who is a patron saint of ecology. St. Francis loved God and all of God's creation.

Tell children how St. Francis gave praise to God for creation, including the sun, stars, moon, water, oceans, animals, and people. He was from a wealthy family but gave everything he had to the poor. His life story reminds us to care for our world and for one another.

Creation craft

Children enjoy making crafts and having something to take home. Show them how to put together a creation craft with a quote from St. Francis of Assisi. This activity for World Day of Prayer for the Care of Creation reminds children to give thanks to God for all creation. On card stock, add the words "All praise be yours, my Lord, through all that you have made." Place the name of St. Francis of Assisi at the bottom.

Each child gets a copy of the quote. Provide creation stickers such as leaves, flowers, animals, and stars so children can make a border around the words. Children can draw small creation pictures instead of using stickers. Encourage them to follow the example of St. Francis of Assisi in giving praise to God for the wonders of our world.

Share resources

God created each one of us and created our world for people to enjoy. Remind children that God gave us our world to share with all people and all generations. We are to take care of creation. It is not right for us to waste or destroy the resources God has given as a gift to all of us.

What we do matters. When we cause harm to our world, people suffer. People living in poverty use less of the earth's resources but are suffering more from the damage done to our environment. When climate change causes drought, many people do not have enough to eat.

Talk with the children about sharing resources on the World Day of Prayer for the Care of Creation and beyond. Stress to children that we can work together. Our God is a God of all people. The time to do something is now.

World Day of Migrants and Refugees

OUR GLOBAL CHURCH OBSERVES THIS SPECIAL DAY ON THE LAST SUNDAY OF SEPTEMBER EACH YEAR. As we focus on World Day of Migrants and Refugees, we remember that each person is created for life with God. We are to treat each person with dignity and respect. Many refugees flee their countries in fear for their lives. We must also be aware of migrant workers who move from place to place, helping with the harvest, and immigrants who seek a better life. In the United States, this special day is part of National Migration Week.

Explore the lives of refugees

Refugees around the world face many problems. Explain to children that refugees must leave everything behind when they flee for their lives. They seek to escape from violence, war, gangs, and poverty. Across the globe, millions of people are on the move every day. Many refugees are children.

Explain that each year, we have a World Day of Migrants and Refugees so we can remember that God created all of us, and we are to help one another on our life journey. We are called to share our blessings with others. Encourage children in your group to pray for refugees and to think of creative solutions to the problems in our world on this day and beyond.

Reach out to refugee children

We are all one people created by God for life with God. Explain this to your group of children. In the New Testament we hear, "Welcome one another, then, as Christ welcomed you" (Romans 15:7). Stress the importance of welcoming newcomers to our country. Suggest that children reach out to new children in their school or neighborhood who are refugees from other countries. In this way we share God's love on World Day of Migrants and Refugees and beyond.

Encourage children to see different cultures as something to be celebrated. We all can learn from one another. Talk about how our different ideas and customs enrich our world, our communities, and our lives. Remind everyone that Jesus came for all people and all nations.

Ideas to help refugee children

- Invite a refugee child to join in a game at recess.
- Say hello to new children at your school.
- Show a refugee child where to sit at lunch and eat with them.
- Learn about customs of other cultures.

Litany prayer for refugees

In some parts of the world, life is very difficult. Remind children that Jesus calls us to be people of compassion. We are also to pray for others on World Day of Migrants and Refugees.

Help children pray a litany prayer for refugees. The catechist is the leader. Ask five children to each read a petition. The rest of the group responds with the refrain, "Lord, hear our prayer."

Litany for refugees

LEADER: Loving God, we come before you today to pray for refugees around the world.

READER 1: For families who face violence:

ALL: ***Lord, hear our prayer.***

READER 2: For people who live in fear each day:

ALL: ***Lord, hear our prayer.***

READER 3: For children who go to bed hungry:

ALL: ***Lord, hear our prayer.***

READER 4: For those who have to leave everything behind:

ALL: ***Lord, hear our prayer.***

READER 5: For refugees who must start a new life:

ALL: ***Lord, hear our prayer.***

LEADER: God of compassion, open our hearts to live in peace and share what we have been given with one another. Amen.

Patron saint of immigrants

St. Frances Cabrini is a patron saint of immigrants. Share her story with children of all ages. She was an amazing woman who grew up in Italy but came to the United States to make life better for Italian immigrants who were living in poverty. She faced many hardships in this new country, but she kept on going.

She started hospitals for the sick and homes for children whose parents had died in the yellow fever epidemic. Tell children that St. Frances loved God with all her heart. She shared the love of Jesus Christ with everyone she met. On World Day of Migrants and Refugees, we are to be people of compassion, as she was. We are to welcome people who are new to our country and seeking a better life.

Books for migrant children

In many areas of our country, migrant workers work long hours to harvest crops each year. Explain to children that workers pick many fruits and vegetables by hand in the hot sun. During this time, children in migrant families may not be able to go to school because they have no way to get there.

We must open our hearts to the needs of others beyond our own neighborhoods. See if your diocese has an outreach program for migrant workers and families. Sometimes there is a reading program for children while their parents work in the fields. Ask the children and families of your group to donate books to the reading program. This is a great way for children to help other children on World Day of Migrants and Refugees.

Pray for refugees around the world

God of all people,
we know that you created each one of us.
May we share what we have been given
and stand up for the rights of others.
On World Day of Migrants and Refugees,
we pray for refugees around the world
who face violence and poverty at home.
Give them the strength to endure
and to remember how much you love them.
May we welcome them with open hearts. Amen.

Respect Life Sunday

WE OBSERVE THIS SPECIAL DAY ON THE FIRST SUNDAY OF OCTOBER. Each human life is valuable because God created each of us. On Respect Life Sunday, we are reminded that all life is sacred, including the lives of the unborn and the elderly. We must support the right of all people to live the life God wants for us. This special day is part of Respect Life month.

Respect all life

All people are created and loved by God. Encourage children to appreciate God's gift of life and honor the lives of others on Respect Life Sunday and beyond. Explain that we are to support life for people of all ages. Stress to children that one person's life does not have more value than another person's. Talk about having respect for different ages and different groups of people.

Show respect for all life

- babies not yet born
- people of all abilities
- those in the hospital
- elderly people
- people of all cultures
- those who are dying

Stress that we are to respect the lives of all people. We are all on this life journey together and must see the good in others.

Saint of courage

St. Margaret of Castello was recently declared a saint. Tell children about this saint and her faith in God. Her life is a good example of why we need Respect Life Sunday. When she was born, Margaret was blind, and her spine curved, which made walking difficult. Her parents hid her away in a room because they were ashamed of her. A priest taught her about Jesus and gave her communion.

She was eventually abandoned by her parents and lived on the street. Local people gave her food. She trusted in God and did not become bitter over how she was treated. She later moved to a convent. Share with children that St. Margaret spent the rest of her life helping others, including children, people who were sick, and the dying. She knew that each person is created and loved by God. Her story reminds us to treat all people with respect. Each human life is valuable.

Give baby gifts

A good project for children on Respect Life Sunday helps new moms living in shelters. Share with children that we can show respect for life by helping others. Local organizations sometimes provide tote bags of baby items for moms in need. These women usually have few resources to provide what is needed for a new baby. Remind children that all of us need help sometimes.

Check with the organization that puts together the tote bags. Items usually include onesies, baby socks, baby hats, blankets, baby wash, and bibs. This project is a great way for children and families to support newborns and their moms who need a helping hand.

Open our hearts litany

On Respect Life Sunday and beyond, we are to encourage children to pray for all human life. Do a litany prayer together to respect the lives of all people. The catechist reads the leader part. Five children each read one of the petitions, and the rest of the group responds with the refrain, "Lord, open our hearts."

Prayer to the God of life

LEADER: God of life, we know that you gave life to each person out of love. We respond to the petitions with "Lord, open our hearts."

READER 1: May we respect all life, especially unborn children:

ALL: ***Lord, open our hearts.***

READER 2: May we treat the elderly with dignity and compassion:

ALL: ***Lord, open our hearts.***

READER 3: May we remember that God created all people:

ALL: ***Lord, open our hearts.***

READER 4: May we realize that the life of each person has value:

ALL: ***Lord, open our hearts.***

READER 5: May we stand up for the right to life for all people:

ALL: ***Lord, open our hearts.***

LEADER: Remember that we are to respect all life and work for the rights of each person. Our God is a God of life, and all that God created is good. Amen.

Respect life resources

Stress to your learners that as followers of Jesus, we are to respect all human life. Remind them that Jesus opened his heart to lepers, people who were blind, sinners, and all people. St. Pope John Paul II told us, "The Gospel of life is at the heart of Jesus' message."

The United States Catholic Bishops have put together posters and ideas that can be used for Respect Life Sunday and throughout the year. See their website (usccb.org). One resource is a prayer to St. Joseph as a defender of life, which reminds us of his example in caring for Jesus and his mother on the trip to Bethlehem and on the flight to Egypt.

Helping hospice

Hospice houses provide a peaceful place in local communities for people at the end of their earthly lives. Explain to children that hospice helps us show respect for those who are dying. People are well cared for, and families and friends can visit.

Invite children and families to donate items from the wish list of a local hospice house for Respect Life Sunday. Items needed include relaxation CDs, playing cards, and even birdseed for bird feeders. In addition, children's books and coloring books with crayons are needed for children who visit. This great project benefits people in our community. It reminds us that all life has value.

Respect life prayer

Lord, giver of life,
open our hearts and our lives
as we celebrate Respect Life Sunday.
Teach us to care about people
of all ages and abilities,
including the unborn and the elderly.
We know that each one of us
is created by you and loved by you
since before we were born.
May we appreciate the gifts
that each person has been given
to share with the world. Amen.

World Mission Sunday

THIS SPECIAL DAY IS CELEBRATED ON THE SECOND-LAST SUNDAY OF OCTOBER. On World Mission Sunday, we remember missionaries who carry the good news of Jesus Christ to people around the world. We pray for missionaries and the people they serve. All of us are called to share the good news of Jesus with others. At Mass on this day, there is a special collection for missions around the world.

Around the world

Create a teaching poster to share with your group when you talk about World Mission Sunday. Print words of Jesus in the middle: "Go into the whole world and proclaim the gospel" (Mark 16:15). Cut out pictures from mission websites. Back pictures with colorful paper and glue them to the poster. Print the name of the country under each picture. Include the United States, because missionaries serve remote areas here.

When you gather with children, explain to them that Jesus calls all of us to share the good news with others. Tell children that when we celebrate World Mission Sunday around the world on the second-last Sunday of October, we are reminded that we are a universal church because Jesus Christ came for all people.

Missionaries at work

Many missionaries—priests, brothers, sisters, and laypeople—share the good news of Jesus Christ with others around the world. They work hard to help people in many ways. Remember missionaries and their example of faith on World Mission Sunday and beyond.

Encourage children pray for the missionaries and the people they serve around the world during the year too. Pray also that we will share the good news with others.

The work of missionaries

- Teach people about Jesus.
- Celebrate Mass.
- Visit and care for the sick.
- Help grow food.
- Celebrate the sacraments.
- Bring hope to people in need.
- Assist people with disabilities.
- Pray with the people.

Patron saint of missions

St. Francis Xavier is one of the patron saints of missions. He was the first Jesuit missionary to share the good news of Jesus Christ beyond Europe. He went to places like India and Japan. Share his example of faith on World Mission Sunday.

Even though he grew up in a noble family, St. Francis Xavier lived among the people he served. He dedicated his life to sharing the gospel with others. One way he helped people learn about the gospels was by putting the words to the tune of popular songs.

Stress to children that we are to share the good news of Jesus Christ too. Ask them to pray for missionaries not only on World Mission Sunday but all through the year.

Go and make disciples

After his resurrection, Jesus sent out his disciples (Matthew 28:16–20). One way to share this story with children is an echo pantomime. Say the words and do the gestures line by line; have the children repeat the words and actions.

Sending forth echo pantomime

The eleven disciples went to the mountain	*walk in place*
as Jesus had told them.	*hands by mouth*
Jesus came to the disciples	*point to palms*
and said to them,	*hands by mouth*
"Go and make disciples of all nations.	*arms outstretched*
Baptize the people	*nod head*
in the name of the Father, the Son, and the Holy Spirit,	*sign of the cross*
and teach them what I taught you.	*point to palms*
And remember, I am with you always."	*hands on heart*

Remind children that all of us are called to live as disciples of Jesus. We are to share the good news of Jesus Christ with others on World Mission Sunday and throughout the year.

World mission rosary

Missionaries bring hope to people's lives around the world. They share the good news of Jesus Christ and serve people in need. It is important for children to know that Jesus came for people of all nations. One way to pray for missions around the world is with a World Mission Rosary.

This is a good activity for children on World Mission Sunday. Explain to children that each decade has a different color of beads and is offered for a different area of our world. For example, the green decade is for Africa. Archbishop Fulton Sheen of New York began the World Mission Rosary. It reminds us to pray for people around the world because we are all brothers and sisters of Christ.

Share the good news

Remind children that since we have been baptized, we are called to joyfully share the good news of Jesus Christ with others on World Mission Sunday and always. Our words and our example of faith show people who Jesus Christ is in our lives.

Explain that by sharing the love of Jesus, we bring hope to the lives of others. Ask children to think of people with whom they might share the good news.

Ways to share the good news of Jesus Christ

- Invite people to Sunday Mass.
- Tell others why Jesus is important in our lives.
- Show respect for people of all cultures.
- Reach out with compassion to those in need.
- Show the love Jesus has for each person.

Pray to the Holy Spirit

Holy Spirit of love,
we pray for people around the world
on this World Mission Sunday and beyond.
May we share with them the gospel message
of the love of Jesus Christ.
Help us support missionaries far from home.
Watch over them and guide them.
We pray also for the people they serve
who want to learn about the love of Jesus.
May we remember that each of us is called
to share the good news of Jesus with others. Amen.

All Saints' Day

On November 1, we honor all the new and old saints who followed Jesus in many different ways. They are examples for our lives of how to love God and serve others. On All Saints' Day, we remember that saints come from every country of the world. They honored God and cared for others in their lives each day. God calls all of us to be saints.

Love God and others

Jesus teaches us what it means to love God and love others. Explain to young people that the example of the saints shows us many ways to do this. Help children become more familiar with the greatest commandment by doing an echo pantomime (based on Mark 12:28–31) for All Saints' Day. The catechist says the words and does the actions line by line. Children echo the words and actions.

The greatest commandment

One day a man asked Jesus,	*nod head*
"Which commandment is first?"	*hold up one finger*
Jesus answered,	*point to palms*
"You shall love the Lord your God	*arms raised high*
with all your heart,	*hands on heart*

and with all your soul,	*arms outstretched*
and with all your mind,	*hands to head*
and with all your strength.	*flex arm muscles*
The second is this:	*hold up two fingers*
Love your neighbor	*arms outstretched*
as yourself."	*hug self*

Jesus showed us by his words and actions how we are to live. We must follow Jesus and share God's love with others. In this way we become saints of God's kingdom.

Live like saints

Pope Francis reminds us that "to be saints is not a privilege for the few, but a vocation for everyone." Share with children that All Saints' Day not only honors the example of the saints but reminds us that God calls all of us to be saints. Talk with children about ways we can do this in our lives.

When we live as disciples of Jesus Christ each day, we live as God created us to be. Jesus shows us the way.

Ways to live as saints

- Praise God each day.
- Help people in need.
- Go to Sunday Mass.
- Love God always.
- See Jesus in other people.
- Forgive other people.
- Pray for the needs of others.
- Learn about God's word.
- Stand up for other people.
- Ask the Holy Spirit for help.

Each of us has a purpose

God created each person for a special purpose. Share this idea with young people. Explain that a person's purpose in life is something only they can do. We were each created to give glory to God and to help one another on our faith journey.

In Scripture we learn, "We know that all things work for good for those who love God, who are called according to his purpose" (Romans 8:28). Explain to children that God gives each of us talents and abilities to share with others. Look around and see ways to share your gifts.

Also share with young people the words of St. John Henry Newman, who said, "God has created me to do him some definite service. He has committed some work to me which he has not committed to another." Explore the idea with children that each of us has a purpose for our lives. On All Saints' Day, we remember that all of us are called to be saints.

Honor new saints

Saints are examples of what it means to trust in God in our lives. Share with children that saints followed the way of Jesus. Saints served God and shared God's love with others. They saw a need and did something about it. A good idea for All Saints' Day is to help children become familiar with some of the saints who have been canonized recently. Encourage children to live lives of faith and service like the saints did. Explain that we can ask saints to pray to God for us.

New saints

St. Alberto Hurtado was a person of compassion for street kids.

St. Dulce Lopes Pontes started a medical clinic for the poor.

St. Josephine Bakhita forgave those who made her a slave.

St. Charles Houben visited the sick and the dying.

St. Kateri Tekakwitha praised God for the wonders of creation.

Encourage children to follow the example of saints old and new and to serve others in the name of Jesus Christ.

Saint statue search

Do a saint search when your group is learning about All Saints' Day. Find statues of saints around your church and classroom area. If your parish or school is named after a saint, find a statue of the patron saint and take children to see it. Talk briefly with young people about why that saint is honored by your parish.

Take a tour of other saint statues too: either in your parish or online. Many parishes have a statue of Mary. If your parish is staffed by a religious order of priests or sisters, see if there is a statue of the founder of that order. Talk about the example of that saint. Be creative. Your parish may have icons of saints or stained-glass windows featuring saints. This saint search keeps children moving and talking about saints.

Pray to be like saints

God of all people,
thank you for the example of saints on All Saints' Day.
We remember that they shared your message of hope and love
with the world in many different ways.
The saints did not have easy lives,
but they trusted in you always.
Show us the way to use our gifts to praise you
and serve others as the saints did. Amen.

World Day of the Poor

Pope Francis declared that this special day be observed on the Thirty-Third Sunday of Ordinary Time. As followers of Jesus Christ, we are to work for justice in our world for all people. Pope Francis reminds us to "reach out to those most in need." On World Day of the Poor, we remember that we are to share the resources of our world with all people. We also value all people as created in the image and likeness of God.

Learn about poverty

Poverty is part of our world today. Explain to children that around the world, many people do not have what they need to live. Let your group know that many children around the world go to bed hungry. Explain that many people are poor through no fault of their own.

Reasons for poverty

- Crops fail due to lack of rain.
- War and violence upend people's lives.
- Illness can lead to job loss.
- Floods destroy homes and businesses.
- Climate change causes disasters.

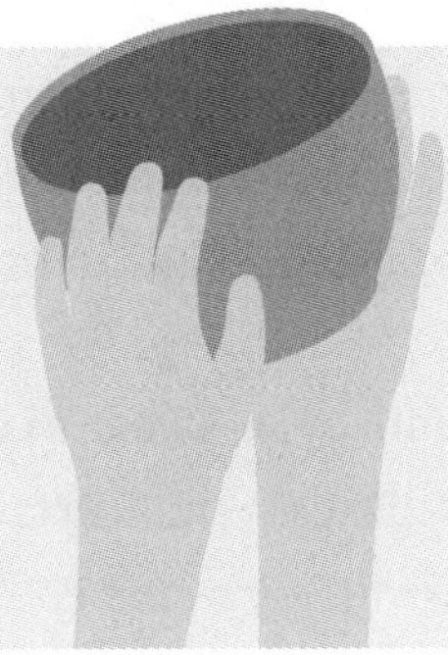

When you gather with your group, explain that each year, the church observes World Day of the Poor to remind us to share the resources of our earth with others. Look online at Catholic Relief Services (crs.org) to see the needs of people around the world. Encourage children to pray for people living in poverty. Stress to your learners that we can start helping people one person, one action, at a time. The need is great. We are to reach out to the poor beyond this one special day.

Serve the poor

The life of Jesus shows us his concern for all people, especially the poor. Explain to children that we can bring hope to people living in poverty in our community with a service project for World Day of the Poor. Emphasize that we can make a difference when we work together. Following are some service ideas. See which one is needed most in your area.

Look online to find other service ideas to help people in need in your community. There are many people who are trying to make life better for others. We can bring hope to the lives of others.

Ways to help the poor

- Provide school supplies for children in low-income areas.
- Give non-perishable food to a food pantry.
- Donate jackets that are too small to a coat drive.
- Offer blankets to an organization that helps the homeless.
- Collect items on a family shelter wish list.

Work of St. Teresa of Calcutta

St. Teresa of Calcutta is a great saint to talk about when you observe World Day of the Poor. This remarkable saint shared God's love with the poor each day. She opened her heart to poor people who were dying alone on the streets of Calcutta, India. Tell children how she went out each day to care for the poorest of the poor. She treated them with kindness and dignity and let them know someone cared.

St. Teresa started a religious order called the Missionaries of Charity to help in her work. Look online to see how her followers serve the poor and suffering around the world. Encourage children to pray for the Missionaries of Charity and for the people they serve.

Welcome home baskets

Some communities have supportive housing that offers homeless people a small apartment to live in and support services. Invite children in your group to reach out to people in supportive housing by collecting items for welcome home baskets. This is a good service idea for World Day of the Poor. It helps turn words into actions.

A welcome home basket is a laundry basket placed in an apartment before a new resident arrives. It has items such as a can opener, dish towels, pot holders, laundry detergent, and other items along with a welcome home card. Check with your local organization for specific needs. This project shows new residents that people care.

Catholic social teaching

We can share with children some important concepts about Catholic social teaching on World Day of the Poor and beyond. A colorful handout for children is available from the U.S. Catholic Bishops' website (usccb.org) and can be printed for children in your group.

This handout explains Catholic social teaching to children in a way they can understand. One of the seven themes is "God wants us to help people who are poor." After reviewing the handout in class, children can take it home to share with their family.

Share world resources

God created our world and its resources to be shared with everyone. Let children know that we are to use just what we need and share the rest with other people. In this way, there is enough for all people and all generations, as God planned for us. St. Ambrose said, "It is not from your own goods that you give to the beggar; it is a portion of his own that you are restoring to him. The Earth belongs to all."

Talk about this quote with children on World Day of the Poor and beyond. Discuss doing things for the good of other people, like Jesus calls us to do. Remind children that the lives of some people are not more valuable than others. God created all of us. Encourage children to be creative thinkers who work toward solving problems of the poor. Each of us can do something.

Pray for the poor

God of love,
open our hearts on this World Day of the Poor
so we may have compassion for people
living in poverty in our world today.
We pray for people who will go to bed hungry tonight
and for all those who struggle to get through each day.
Help us to follow Jesus in caring about the poor
and to remember that you created all of us. Amen.

Thanksgiving Day

THIS SPECIAL DAY IS CELEBRATED IN THE UNITED STATES ON THE FOURTH THURSDAY OF NOVEMBER. We pause to remember how early settlers and Native Americans celebrated the first Thanksgiving together. They gave thanks to God because they had made it through the harsh winter. Thanksgiving is an opportunity for all of us to give thanks to God for our many blessings. Everything we have is a gift given to us with love by God. We remember that God calls us to share our blessings with others.

Give thanks to God

God gives us many gifts. Encourage your group of children to think about giving thanks to God at Thanksgiving. This is a good opportunity to focus on positive things in life. Ask children to brainstorm things for which they give thanks to God.

Give each child a half sheet of paper with the short side at the top. Children print the words "Thank you, God" at the top. Then they print the numbers 1 to 10 down the left side. Ask children to write down some things for which they are thankful. Suggest that they take home their lists to remember to give thanks to God each day.

Give praise with psalms

The words of the psalms in the Bible have helped people give praise and thanks to God for thousands of years. Explore this idea with children. Explain that we join our voices with people all over the world when we pray the psalms.

Show children how to make a psalm craft to give thanks to God at Thanksgiving. There are many psalm verses for children to use.

Psalms of praise

- **Give thanks to the Lord** (PSALM 107:1)
- **Great are the works of the Lord** (PSALM 111:2)
- **You are my God, I give you thanks** (PSALM 118:28)
- **I will praise your name forever and ever** (PSALM 145:2)
- **Sing to the Lord with thanksgiving** (PSALM 147:7)

Ask each child to choose a psalm verse. Have copies of psalm verses for younger children. Let older children write out a verse with markers. Then younger and older children glue the verse to a half sheet of orange card stock. They put fall foam leaf stickers around the verse as a border. Children take home their craft to remember to give thanks to God at Thanksgiving.

Thank-you cards

Thanksgiving is a great time to thank not only God but the people around us. Invite children to make thanksgiving cards to give to people who have been a blessing in their lives. Talk with children about who this might be. Children learn from one another's ideas.

People who would appreciate a thank-you card

- A grandparent who is always willing to listen.
- A teacher who takes extra time for you.
- A family friend who has helped your family.
- A doctor or nurse who took care of you.

Provide manila drawing paper and markers for children to make one-of-a-kind cards. Show them how to fold the paper in half. On the front of the card, children print "Happy Thanksgiving" and decorate it. Inside, they write a message of thanks and print or sign their name. Have enough supplies so children can make more than one card if they choose.

Pray a psalm with gestures

Praise God with children using the words of Psalm 92:2–3, 5–6, with actions. This guides children in praising God with their whole body. This psalm reminds them that we are to praise God in the day and in the night. The catechist says the words and gestures, and children echo line by line.

It is good to give thanks to the Lord,	*arms over head*
to sing praise to your name, Most High,	*hands by mouth*
To proclaim your love at daybreak,	*hands on heart*
your faithfulness in the night...	*hands next to head*
For you make me jubilant, Lord,	*arms over head*
by your deeds;	*nod head yes*
at the works of your hands	*psalms up in front*
I shout for joy.	*hands by mouth*
How great are your works, Lord!	*arms outstretched*

In this way, children give thanks together to God and remember all that God has done for us. This psalm helps us lift up our hearts to God, who loves us without end. It is a great psalm to use to give thanks to our God at Thanksgiving and all through the year.

Fall leaves for seniors

Children enjoy making colorful fall leaf decorations to give to people at a community senior center. These centers provide low-cost lunches to area residents. Decorations for a fall lunch are placed at each person's place setting. After the lunch, seniors take home their individual decorations.

Show children how to cut out six-inch maple leaves from colorful craft foam using a pattern. Leaves can be precut for younger children. Children add foam leaf stickers in fall colors such as yellow, orange, and red. Each child needs to make several leaves. These colorful leaf decorations help children share the joy of fall and Thanksgiving time with others.

Pray to an amazing God

Amazing God,
we give you thanks for all the gifts
you have given us out of love.
We thank you for the beauty of our world
and the people who share our lives.
Most of all, we thank you
for your unending love for each of us.
May we remember the needs of others this Thanksgiving
and reach out to them. Amen.

First Sunday of Advent

THIS SPECIAL DAY IS CELEBRATED FOUR WEEKS BEFORE CHRISTMAS EACH YEAR (SOMETIMES IT FALLS AT THE END OF NOVEMBER). The First Sunday of Advent is the beginning of the church year. As we journey together through Advent, we move toward Bethlehem. We wait in hope during the season of Advent to celebrate the birth of Jesus at Christmas. We are people of hope because we know that the child in the manger is Jesus Christ our Lord. God's promise to the people was fulfilled in a way no one would have expected.

Advent is here

The First Sunday of Advent starts the four-week season that leads up to Christmas. The word Advent means "coming." Explain to children that we wait to celebrate the coming of Jesus at Christmas. We light one candle on the Advent wreath on the first Sunday. Then each week we light one more candle as Christmas gets closer. Tell children that Advent wreaths are lit at Mass and sometimes people have Advent wreaths at home.

Share with your group of children that Advent is a time of hope and a time of sharing with others. We pray for the needs of other people, too, such as the poor and refugees. Stress that we get ready for Christmas in our hearts and our lives.

Questions about Advent

When does the season of Advent start?
(First Sunday of Advent)

How many candles are lit that day? *(one)*

How many weeks does Advent last? *(four)*

Who can we pray for during Advent? *(the poor, refugees)*

What are we waiting for during Advent?
(Jesus to be born at Christmas)

Advent actions

As the First Sunday of Advent approaches, encourage children to be people of kindness to others during the Advent season. Stress that each of us can do something for someone else. Help children think of ways to do this.

Advent actions

- Talk to a child who seems lonely.
- Say hello to an elderly person at Mass.
- Donate a new toy to a children's shelter.
- Ask another child to join your game at recess.
- Visit an elderly person in assisted living.
- Pray for refugees who are new to our country.

Any of these ideas is a great way to get started helping others. Explore with children how each of us can make a difference during Advent. God sends us to help others.

Come, Lord Jesus

We use words from Scripture as a prayer during Advent as we wait to celebrate the coming of Jesus at Christmas. Tell children that the words "Come, Lord Jesus" are one of the last prayers in the Bible.

These words are found in Revelation 22:20. Pope Francis reminds us that this simple prayer can be said often during Advent.

This prayer reminds us of what we are waiting for during Advent. We wait to celebrate the coming of Jesus, the Savior of all people. "Come, Lord Jesus" is a simple daily prayer for all of us as we prepare our hearts and our lives during Advent. Share with children that it is important to pray during the Advent season and beyond. Prayer is part of our friendship with Jesus.

A saint for Advent

In the Advent season, we celebrate the life of St. Virginia Centurione on December 15. Tell children that this saint shared God's love with others. She reached out a helping hand to people who were sick, refugees, the hungry, and children without families. When she saw a need, she did something about it. We can do that too.

Ask young people to share God's love with others during Advent like St. Virginia did. Encourage them to be kind to one person each day until Christmas. This might be talking to someone who seems sad, sharing play equipment, or praying for someone in need. In this way, they share God's love with others like this saint did. This is a great way to get ready to celebrate Christmas.

Be an Advent angel

Children can be Advent angels and bring hope to the lives of sick children. Tell your group that they can make Christmas tree craft kits for children at the local children's hospital. This provides a fun activity for sick children to do in their rooms.

Show children in your group how to assemble craft kits. They put a precut eight-inch Christmas tree shape in a quart storage bag. Then they add Christmas stickers for tree decorations and simple directions.

Children in the hospital attach the stickers to the tree to make a colorful Christmas decoration for their room or door. This gives them something to do while they are getting the medical care they need.

Pray to wait in hope

God of heaven and earth,
during this season of Advent
we wait in joyful hope to celebrate
the coming of Jesus at Christmas.
May Advent be a time of new beginnings
as we start a new church year.
May we share your love with others
as we walk this Advent season together. Amen.

Feast of Our Lady of Guadalupe

WE CELEBRATE THIS BEAUTIFUL FEAST DAY ON DECEMBER 12 EACH YEAR. On the feast of Our Lady of Guadalupe, we honor Mary, who appeared to a humble man in Mexico and brought hope to the Native people who were suffering. Our Lady of Guadalupe let the people know that God loved them. This day is a time of hope and of rejoicing. We remember that God loves each of us.

Share the story

The story of Our Lady of Guadalupe is a great one to share with children. Tell them that Juan Diego lived in Mexico at a time when people from Spain had conquered the area. The Native people were badly treated and lived in poverty. One day, as Juan was walking to Mass, he heard someone call his name. He was amazed to see a beautiful lady "clothed with the sun."

Mary told Juan that God had not forgotten the Native people. She asked Juan to go to the bishop and request that a church be built where she was standing. This was not easy for Juan, but he went. The bishop listened and told him to ask Mary for a sign. Mary had Juan gather roses that were blooming on a hillside where roses did not usually grow. When Juan opened his cloak to show the roses to the bishop, a likeness of Mary was on the inside!

Explain to children that the Shrine of Our Lady of Guadalupe was built, and the cloak with the picture of Mary is still displayed there. Millions of people visit this shrine each year. Mary's appearance reminds us to treat people of all cultures with respect.

Respect all cultures

Teach young people how the appearance of Our Lady of Guadalupe to Juan Diego reminds us that it is important to treat people of all cultures with respect. God created all of us and loves each one of us. We are to bring hope in God to the lives of others.

Encourage children to learn about cultures other than their own. Remind them that we are to stand up for the rights of others and work for justice for all people. Stress that the lives of one group of people are not more important than those of another group. God created all of us.

Our Lady of Guadalupe echo pantomime

Children enjoy doing an echo pantomime about Our Lady of Guadalupe. The catechist says each line and does the actions. Children then echo the words and gestures line by line.

The story of Our Lady of Guadalupe

One day, Juan Diego was walking	*walk in place*
when he heard someone call his name.	*hands behind ears*
It was Mary, the mother of Jesus.	*nod head*
She wanted all people to remember	*arms out at sides*
that God loves them always.	*hug self*
She asked Juan to go to the bishop	*walk in place*
and ask him to build a church.	*hands by mouth*
The bishop asked for a sign,	*nod head*
so Mary told Juan to gather roses	*arms out*
where they did not usually grow.	*shrug shoulders*
Juan went back to the bishop	*walk in place*
and opened his cloak to give the roses.	*open arms*
But there was Mary's picture on his cloak!	*nod head*
The church was built,	*pretend to pound*
and many people come there to pray.	*fold hands*

Litany to Our Lady of Guadalupe

Explain to children that we can ask Mary to pray for us to her Son, Jesus. One way to do this is with a litany prayer to Our Lady of Guadalupe. The catechist is the leader. Ask five children to each read a petition. All children respond, "Our Lady of Guadalupe, pray for us."

LEADER: We gather together to honor Our Lady of Guadalupe. Her appearance reminds us that God loves people of all cultures and calls us to do the same.

READER 1: May we treat people of all cultures with respect:

ALL: ***Our Lady of Guadalupe, pray for us.***

READER 2: May we open our hearts to the needs of others:

ALL: ***Our Lady of Guadalupe, pray for us.***

READER 3: May we remember how much God loves each of us:

ALL: ***Our Lady of Guadalupe, pray for us.***

READER 4: May we bring hope to the lives of other people:

ALL: ***Our Lady of Guadalupe, pray for us.***

READER 5: May we honor Mary as the mother of all people:

ALL: ***Our Lady of Guadalupe, pray for us.***

LEADER: Always remember to treat all people with dignity and respect. May we work for justice and walk in peace. Amen.

Pray to Our Lady of Guadalupe

Our Lady of Guadalupe,
you came to bring a message of hope
to Native people who were suffering.
Thank you for helping us remember
to treat all people with respect.
Pray for us to your Son, Jesus,
that we may bring hope to the lives of others
during Advent and always. Amen.

Christmas Day

We celebrate this wonderful day as we sing the Gloria and give glory to our God. On Christmas Day, we find the true gift of Christmas, which is Jesus Christ our Lord. We rejoice because God has fulfilled the promise to the people in a way we never could have expected. Jesus came for all people: past, present, and future. The season of Christmas that follows this day should make a difference in our lives as we share hope in our Savior with others.

Give glory to God

At Christmas, we sing out, "Glory to God in the highest!" (Luke 2:14). Explain to children that these words of the angels to the shepherds are our words too. Jesus Christ came for all people, all nations, all cultures. We lift up our voices, our hearts, and our lives to God who loves us without end.

Share with children that we must make room in our hearts and our lives to celebrate what Christmas means. We are to be people who praise God and share with others. It is important to remember that Christmas is a beginning and not an end. Christmas day begins, not ends, the season of Christmas.

Create a heart tree

In the gathering area, set up a tree and invite children to decorate it with heart ornaments. This helps them remember that Christmas is all about God's love for us and sharing God's love with others. Explain to children that heart ornaments can be made in many ways: cutting hearts out of patterned scrapbook paper, using self-stick craft jewels on card stock hearts, decorating felt hearts from kits, or creating mosaic hearts by sticking squares of red and green craft foam to hearts.

Children punch a hole in the top of their ornament and use red and green yarn to make hangers. Be sure each child's name is on the back of their ornament. If you are doing a tree with other classes, ask each group to make a separate type of ornament. Remind children to share God's love at Christmas time and throughout the year.

Stocking project

Christmas is a time to share the love of God with others. Encourage children and families to reach out to people in need in the community. One way is to provide filled Christmas stockings for children living in low-income housing.

Ask your children to bring in donations of items for the stockings, such as coloring books, crayons, toy cars, card games, and candy canes. Get Christmas stockings in bulk. Provide the opportunity for older children to fill the stockings. Have adults help to be sure that only one of each item is in the stocking. This project brings hope to the lives of children who receive the stockings at Christmas.

Christmas season saint

One of the saints we celebrate during the Christmas season is St. Caterina Volpicelli. Her feast day is December 28. As a teen, Caterina liked to go to parties with her friends. Then she decided to take time to share the love of Jesus Christ with others. She helped people who were sick during the cholera epidemic.

We can help sick people also. Talk with children about ways to comfort the sick such as making get well cards, calling someone who is sick, or reading a story to a young child who is not feeling well. Encourage children to share their own ideas too.

Tell children that time off from school during Christmas vacation is also a good time to do a project for the sick with friends or family members. They could make placemats for a meals on wheels organization that delivers meals to the sick, or donate cans of soup to the food pantry. Their family might visit a relative in a care center. Let children know that we can also pray for people in our parish who are sick or people on the news who are injured. Everyone can do something.

Acts of caring

- Thank someone who has been kind.
- Play a game with a younger child.
- Tell someone to have a good day.
- Pray for children who go to bed hungry.
- Make a card for a sick person.
- Hold the door for someone at Mass.
- Let another person go ahead of you.
- Draw a picture and give it away.
- Listen to someone who is sad.
- Do a chore for someone.
- Share a book or game.
- Tell someone God loves them.

Twelve days of caring

Christmas season begins on Christmas day. We celebrate the birth of Jesus and all that the coming of Jesus means for the world. Explain to children that the twelve days of the Christmas season are from Christmas Day to January 6, the feast of the Epiphany. Encourage children to live the twelve days of Christmas by doing an act of caring each day to share the joy of Christmas with others

Invite children in your group to think of their own ideas too. By being kind and reaching out to others, we live the message of love of the Christmas season.

Praise God at Christmas

God of glory,
we thank you for sending Jesus Christ to us
as the light of the world and the light of our lives
on the first Christmas many years ago.
We celebrate your unending love for us
and ask you to help us share that love with others.
May we reach out a helping hand
not just at Christmas but all through the year. Amen.

World Day of Peace

ON JANUARY 1 EACH YEAR, WE CELEBRATE THIS SPECIAL DAY. World Day of Peace reminds us that Jesus calls us be peacemakers and live in peace with one another. We are to be people of forgiveness and mercy toward others. Jesus showed us how to do this by his words and actions. God calls us to work for peace in the choices we make. We must value all people as created in the image and likeness of God. We can do this with the help of the Holy Spirit in our lives.

Live as peacemakers

- Forgive someone who hurt you.
- Do not push someone who pushes you.
- Let go of old hurts.
- Reply to angry words with calm words.
- Ask forgiveness of others.
- Learn about other cultures.
- Listen to the ideas of other people.
- Pray for victims of violence.

Be peacemakers

Stress to children that God wants us to work toward peace in our families, our communities, and our world. Each year we celebrate World Day of Peace to remind us to walk in peace. Explore with children the idea that we can begin by focusing on one person and one action at a time.

Explain that we are to be people who forgive others and who do not hold grudges. We are called to be people of peace each day. Talk about ways to be peacemakers.

Explore with children in your group that we are to work together for the rights of all people. Individually and together, we can make a difference.

God created all people

The U.S. Catholic Bishops' letter "Open Wide Our Hearts" helps people understand that God created all of us as one human race. Share this quote with children: "Racism occurs because a person ignores the fundamental truth that, because all humans share a common origin, they are all brothers and sisters, all equally made in the image of God."

A copy of this document is found on the U.S. Catholic Bishops' website (usccb.org). Lesson plans on racism are also found there to use with children in your group. Stress to children that all people are created and loved by God. We are to value the lives of all people and treat others with dignity and respect. If we do not act when we see people being treated unfairly, we fail to live as Jesus teaches us.

Even though you might not meet with your group of learners on World Day of Peace, you can teach them about working for peace in our lives and our world when you do meet. Peace is for every day of our lives. Explain to children that there will only be peace in our world when we realize that we are all brothers and sisters in Jesus Christ.

Song of hope

Children feel helpless and afraid when they see violence happening in their own communities and around the world. We need to share hope in God with children when we teach them about World Day of Peace.

One way to do this is with the wonderful song "Hold on to Love" by Jesse Manibusan. The lyrics and the song are available on YouTube. The song can also be downloaded from Oregon Catholic Press (ocp.org). Play the song and let children listen to it. Talk about the message. Ask children which words were important. Then play the song again and ask children to sing the refrain.

This song gives hope to young people and all of us in difficult times. Stress to children that when we feel that violence is all around us, we are able to "Hold on to Love." We know that God's love is all around us. The words of this song speak to the hearts and lives of young people and all of us.

Share a true story

Read a great book to children about peace that is a true story. *Wangari's Trees of Peace* by Jeanette Winter is about a girl from Africa who planted trees to replace ones that had been cut down. In doing so, she brings hope to her village. Wangari Maathai won a Nobel Peace Prize for the difference she made in the lives of others.

Tell children that this true story reminds us of what one person can do. When you talk about World Day of Peace, this book inspires us by the example of one person who made a difference. Encourage children to think how they might make a difference even in a small way. Each of us can do something.

Saint for peace

The story of St. Oscar Romero is a good one to share with older children on World Day of Peace. He was a priest who served people living in poverty in El Salvador. He worked for justice and called for peace in the name of Jesus Christ. St. Oscar said, "We must continually say no to violence and yes to peace."

Tell children that he had the courage to speak out against violence to others on the radio so everyone could hear. As a result, he was killed as he celebrated Mass for the people. The example of St. Oscar reminds us that Jesus calls all of us to work for peace.

Pray to live in peace

God of hope,
help us to live in peace in our world
on World Day of Peace and always.
We know that you created all people out of love.
May we stand up for the rights of others
and be peacemakers in our lives.
Guide us to work together for the good of all people
in our communities, our nation, and our world. Amen.

Epiphany of the Lord

THIS SPECIAL DAY CELEBRATES THE MAGI WHO TRAVELED FROM THE EAST, FOLLOWING A STAR. They came to honor Jesus. Epiphany of the Lord is observed on January 6, which is twelve days after Christmas. It may also be celebrated on the Sunday after January 1 so more people are able to participate in the celebration. We think there were three magi because the gospel mentions three gifts. We are to be like the magi and follow the star of Jesus in our lives wherever it may lead us.

The story of the magi

The gospel for the feast of the Epiphany of the Lord is Matthew 2:1–12. Share the story of the magi from far away who saw the star of Jesus. Explain that sometimes they are called the wise men. They knew that something important had happened, so they followed the star. Tell children that we assume there were three magi because the gospel mentions three gifts.

Ask questions to help children understand the story of the magi

Where was Jesus born? *(Bethlehem)*

Who was looking for Jesus? *(magi)*

Where did the magi come from? *(the East)*

What did they follow? *(a star)*

Who did they find? *(Jesus, Mary, and Joseph)*

Who did Jesus come for? *(all people)*

Point out to children that other people must have seen the bright star. We don't know why they did not follow it. The magi were open to God working in their lives. Remind children that we, too, must make time for Jesus and follow where God leads us. Tell children that this gospel reminds us that Jesus came for all people, all nations, all cultures.

Gifts for Jesus

Keep a nativity scene on display through Epiphany. Add figures of the three magi after Christmas. Place a basket in front of the scene. Then explain to children that each of the magi brought a gift to Jesus. We can give gifts from our hearts to Jesus at Epiphany.

Encourage them to think of gifts from their hearts. Talk about some ideas to get children started.

Ask each child to cut out a four-inch star from yellow paper using a pattern. Explain that each child prints the gift he or she will give Jesus on their star. Tell children that they do not have to write a lot of words. They can simply put "be kind," "forgive," or "share," for example. Then children come forward and place their star in the basket in front of the nativity scene. Before children leave for the day, remind them to do their gift for Jesus.

Gifts to give to Jesus

- Share with others.
- Talk to someone who is sad.
- Do a random act of kindness.
- Say something positive.
- Treat other people with respect.
- Forgive someone.
- Be kind to another child.
- Thank God for sending us Jesus.

Light litany prayer

Gather children for prayer to remind them that we are to follow the light of Christ in our lives, as the magi did. Tell children that with God, all things are possible. God hears our prayers. This litany prayer can be prayed even after the celebration of Epiphany. We are called to seek Jesus in our lives always.

The catechist can be the leader. Ask five children to each read a petition. All children pray the response together.

Litany of light

LEADER: We celebrate today that Jesus came for all people. We are to follow the light of Jesus Christ in our lives now and always.

READER 1: When life seems difficult:

ALL: ***May we follow the light of Jesus.***

READER 2: When we don't know what to do:

ALL: ***May we follow the light of Jesus.***

READER 3: When things go wrong:

ALL: ***May we follow the light of Jesus.***

READER 4: When another child seems sad or lonely:

ALL: ***May we follow the light of Jesus.***

READER 5: When we see an elderly person who needs help:

ALL: ***May we follow the light of Jesus.***

LEADER: Lord Jesus, help us to live in your light and follow you always. We know that with you, all things are possible. Amen.

Follow the star of Jesus

Encourage younger children to follow the star of Jesus in their lives after they leave the group. Create a simple take-home project. Draw the outline of a large star on a piece of paper, and under it print "Star of Jesus." Run off a copy for each child. Put self-stick stars in self-sealing snack bags for each child. Any kind of star stickers is fine, though very small stars are difficult for little fingers. Also include simple directions so families can encourage children.

Have everything ready when you gather with the children. Talk about doing good deeds for others. Invite them to take home a star of Jesus page and a sticker bag. Explain that each time they do something kind, they can put a star on the star of Jesus. If they run out of stars, they can simply draw one. This is a great Epiphany project for young children.

Pray to follow the light of Jesus

Jesus, Light of the World,
we know that the magi from the East
went on a long journey following the star.
Help us to look for your light
in our lives at Epiphany and always.
May we share your light with others
and remember you came for all people. Amen.

Ordinary Time

THIS SEASON IS A TIME TO LIVE WHAT WE BELIEVE AS DISCIPLES OF JESUS CHRIST. We give praise to our God who is Father, Son, and Holy Spirit. We let the Holy Spirit work in our lives. Ordinary Time is the longest season of the church year. It is in two parts: one before Ash Wednesday, and the other after the Easter season. There is nothing ordinary about Ordinary Time. The name refers to counted time, such as the Second Sunday of Ordinary Time.

Come and see echo pantomime

One of the wonderful gospel stories we hear at Mass during Ordinary Time invites us to come and see what following Jesus is all about (John 1:35–42). Share an echo pantomime of this gospel with children. Say the words and do the actions line by line. Ask children to echo the words and actions.

Come and see echo pantomime

John was with two of his disciples	*hold up two fingers*
when Jesus walked by.	*walk in place*
John sent the two to follow Jesus.	*point*
They asked him,	*nod*
"Where are you staying?"	*hands by mouth*
Jesus said, "Come and see."	*wave arm*
So they followed Jesus.	*walk in place*
Later, Andrew told his brother,	*hands by mouth*
"We have found the Messiah."	*raise arms*
Andrew brought Simon to see Jesus.	*walk in place*
Jesus said, "You will be called Peter."	*nod head*
Jesus calls us to "Come and see."	*wave arm*
We are called to follow Jesus	*walk in place*
and tell others about him.	*hands by mouth*

Children learn by being actively involved. Young people remember more of what they do than what they hear. Echo pantomimes are a great way to share gospel stories with children.

Walk with Jesus

Remind children to live the gospels during Ordinary Time and always. Talk with them about ways to follow Jesus in our lives as gospel people. We must guide children to make the connection between their lives and the gospels.

Ways to follow Jesus

- Give praise to God.
- Serve others with love.
- Tell other people about Jesus.
- Pray for the needs of others.
- Live our purpose.
- Let the Holy Spirit work in us.

Encourage children to think of their own ideas too. Each of us has different gifts to share. Hearing the ideas of others catches their attention and helps children learn from one another. In this way, we multiply the learning.

Make a patterned cross

During Ordinary Time, encourage children to follow the way of Jesus in all they do. Show them how to make a patterned cross to display at home as a reminder to walk with Jesus.

Children cut out individual crosses from green patterned scrapbook paper. Then guide them to place their crosses on half-sheets of green card stock. Show children how to cut out a cross larger than the patterned cross. They then glue the patterned cross to the larger green cross.

Let children know that the crosses are green because that is the color of Ordinary Time. Encourage each child to display their individual cross at home as a reminder to live as disciples of Jesus each day during Ordinary Time and throughout the year.

Live in faith, hope, and love

We are called to be disciples of Jesus Christ and live in faith, hope, and love during the season of Ordinary Time and beyond. We should focus on living as disciples of Jesus Christ each day. Talk about ways to live in faith, hope, and love.

Live in faith

We are to have faith in God who is always with us and loves us with an unending love. Explain to children that we are to give glory to God—Father, Son, and Holy Spirit—by our words and actions. We are called to trust in God even when life is difficult. Talk about ways to live in faith, hope, and love during the season of Ordinary Time.

WAYS TO LIVE IN FAITH

Offer each day to God.

Be people of compassion.

Share stories of Jesus with others.

Live in hope

We are to be people who hope in God and hope in the future. We know that God created us for life with others. We share hope in God with others as we walk together on our faith journey. Talk about being people of hope.

WAYS TO LIVE IN HOPE

Know that God is always with you.

Look for the good in the world.

Share hope in Jesus with other people.

Live in love

We are to love God and love one another. Tell children that we are to open our hearts and our lives to the needs of other people, as Jesus did. God created us to reach out a helping hand to others. We are a community of God's people. Talk about living with love of God and others.

WAYS TO LIVE IN LOVE

Open your heart to how much God loves you.

Realize that God loves you always.

hare God's love with others.

Encourage children to share their own ideas about living in faith, hope, and love. Children learn from one another.

Kids care project

Provide a way for children in your group to reach out to other children during Ordinary Time. One kids care project is collecting supplies needed for children at an emergency shelter. This is where children go to stay safe when they cannot be cared for at home. These shelters provide everything for children who often arrive with few possessions.

See what your local emergency children's shelter needs. Items usually in short supply include night-lights, toothbrushes and toothpaste, socks, and stuffed animals. Everything should be new. Invite your children and families to donate items. This project helps kids open their hearts to other children during Ordinary Time. Remind them that we all need help sometimes.

Pray during Ordinary Time

Jesus, Lord of all people,
guide us to live always as your disciples
and follow in your footsteps
during the season of Ordinary Time and beyond.
Help us to live in faith, walk in hope,
and share your love with others. Amen.

Sunday of the Word of God

THIS DAY REMINDS US THAT GOD SPEAKS TO ALL GENERATIONS THROUGH THE BIBLE AND THE HOLY SPIRIT. "When the sacred Scriptures are read in the Church, God himself speaks to his people, and Christ, present in his word, proclaims the Gospel" (*General Instruction of the Roman Missal*, no. 29). We are to live what we hear proclaimed in Scripture because it is the word of God speaking to us. Sunday of the Word of God is celebrated on the Third Sunday of Ordinary Time.

Living the Gospels

Each Sunday at Mass, we hear the gospel proclaimed. Explain to your learners that after Mass, we are to go and live what we have heard. Sunday of the Word of God is a good time to remember the importance of Scripture in our lives.

Pope Francis started the special observance of this Sunday of the Word of God. He said, "The relationship between the Risen

Lord, the community of believers and sacred Scripture is essential to our identity as Christians." Share this quote with your group and talk about it.

Scripture search

Spending time with the word of God helps us remember what life is about. Stress to children that whether we hear the word, read it, share it, live it, or pray about it, we know God is the reason for our lives.

Help older children do a Scripture search for Sunday of the Word of God. Divide children into groups of three and give each group a Bible verse to look up. Be sure each child has a Bible to use for this activity. Encourage them to help one another: in their group, they find the verse and write it down. Then ask a volunteer in each group to read the verse aloud. Talk briefly about each verse.

Scripture search

- **You will be my people, and I will be your God** (EZEKIEL 36:28)
- **Trust in the Lord with all your heart** (PROVERBS 3:5)
- **Blessed are the peacemakers** (MATTHEW 5:9)
- **The same Lord is Lord of all** (ROMANS 10:12)
- **Your every act should be done with love** (1 CORINTHIANS 16:14)

Tell children that if they do not have a Bible at home, the website of the United States Catholic Bishops (usccb.org) has a copy of the New American Bible. With the online Bible, you can look up verses more easily.

Love one another echo pantomime

Children need to know that we are to live the word of God. One way is to do an echo pantomime of a gospel. This is a good activity for Sunday of the Word of God. This echo pantomime is based on John 13:34–35, where Jesus calls us to love one another. Say the words and do the actions line by line. Children echo the words and actions.

Love one another echo pantomime

The night before he died,	*point to palms*
Jesus said to his disciples,	*hands by mouth*
"I give you a new commandment:	*nod head*
love one another.	*open arms wide*
As I have loved you,	*hands on heart*
so you also should love one another.	*open arms wide*
This is how people will know	*nod head*
that you are my disciples,	*walk in place*
if you have love for one another."	*open arms wide*
Jesus calls us to love others	*hands on heart*
by our words and actions.	*nod head*

Point out to children that these words of Jesus are a call to action. We are to love others in the name of Jesus. Stress that Jesus came for all people, all cultures, and all races. Activities such as echo pantomimes help children understand that we are to live the gospels in our lives.

Caring actions

Remind young people that we are to live God's word in what we do and say. Pope Francis started the Sunday of the Word of God so we can remember the importance of Scripture in our lives. As disciples of Jesus, we are to care about others as he did. Talk with children about ways to help other people.

Encourage children to open their hearts to the needs of others. Point out that Jesus calls us to put our faith into action.

Care about others

- Make a thank-you card for someone.
- Ask a new child to sit by you at lunch.
- Open the door for someone who is elderly.
- Donate school supplies to a community project.
- Pray for people suffering from floods or fire.
- Say "Have a good day" to someone after Mass.

A saint who shared the word of God

Explore with children how St. Anthony of Padua brought joy to people as he shared the word of God with them. St. Anthony reminded people how much our God loves us. He encouraged people to live the gospel each day.

Share with children that St. Anthony was a priest who lived long ago in the town of Padua, Italy. People liked to hear him teach about Scripture. Some days the crowd had to move outside the church to make room for everyone who wanted to hear him. His example reminds us to share the word of God with other people. He is a good saint to learn about for Sunday of the Word of God.

Personalize Scripture

Stress to your learners that God speaks to us through Scripture. God knows each of us and calls us by name. Print copies of the individual Bible verses below, adding a line at the beginning of the verse. Children choose a verse and print their first name at the beginning of it. An example is "Trent, I have called you by name: you are mine." Older children can write their name at the beginning and then copy a verse from a whiteboard.

Scripture verses to personalize

__________, the Lord, your God, is with you. JOSHUA 1:9

__________, trust in the Lord with all your heart. PROVERBS 3:5

__________, I have called you by name: you are mine. ISAIAH 43:1

__________, call to me, and I will answer you. JEREMIAH 33:3

__________, nothing will be impossible for God. LUKE 1:37

Children decorate their verse with colored markers. This activity shows children that the word of God speaks to each of us. This is a good way to celebrate Sunday of the Word of God with all ages. Invite children to share their personalized verse with their families.

Pray to open our hearts

Holy Spirit,
we give you thanks for the gift of Scripture,
passed on through generations in the church.
Open our hearts to hear your word in our lives
on the Sunday of the Word of God and always.
May we live as disciples of Jesus Christ each day
and share the good news with others. Amen.

World Day of the Sick

THIS SPECIAL DAY IS OBSERVED ON FEBRUARY 11. We remember people who are ill in our world and in need of care. The gospels have many examples of how Jesus cared about those who were sick. On World Day of the Sick and beyond, we are to follow the example of Jesus and open our hearts to the needs of people who are sick or injured, are in the hospital, have mental illness, are having medical tests, or are undergoing treatment. We walk with Jesus in caring for the sick.

Our Lady of Lourdes

The date for World Day of the Sick was chosen because February 11 is the day we honor Our Lady of Lourdes. Tell children the story. One day, when she was 14 years old, a girl named Bernadette went out to gather firewood near her home in Lourdes, France. She saw a light and then a young woman holding a rosary. It was Mary, the mother of Jesus.

Explain to children that Bernadette saw Mary many more times too. Our Lady asked Bernadette to dig in the mud. Bernadette found a natural spring. Some of the sick people who came to the spring were healed. Today, many people still travel to Lourdes hoping to be healed.

Jesus heals the sick

When we observe World Day of the Sick, we remember the example of Jesus healing people who were sick. Jesus shows us that each person matters. Share the account of Jesus healing the sick from Luke 4:40: "At sunset, all who had people sick with various diseases brought them to him. He laid his hands on each of them and cured them."

Jesus was a person of compassion. Explain to your learners that God wants us to be people of compassion too. We are to care about people like Jesus did. Our words and actions can bring comfort to people when they are sick.

Healing two blind men echo pantomime

Jesus cared about the sick and blessed the lives of those who came to him. Explore a gospel story about Jesus healing people for World Day of the Sick. Share with children the story of Jesus healing two blind men (Matthew 9:27–31). Then do an echo pantomime with your learners so they remember the story. Explain that the gesture used for Jesus is to point to the nail holes in both hands.

Healing two blind men echo pantomime

As Jesus was walking,	*walk in place*
two blind men followed.	*hands over eyes*
They asked Jesus to have pity on them.	*fold hands in prayer*
They shouted, "Lord, have mercy on us!"	*hands by mouth*
Jesus asked the blind men,	*point to palms*
"Do you think I can do this?"	*palms up*
He said to them,	*point to palms*
"Let it be done according to your faith,"	*fold hands in prayer*
and he healed them of their blindness.	*nod head yes*
They went and told everyone	*hands by mouth*
what Jesus had done.	*point to palms*

This story reminds us of the love and mercy Jesus has for all of us, especially the sick. Talk with your group about what happened in this gospel story. Stress to children that we are to have faith in Jesus Christ too. We can be people of compassion for the sick, like Jesus was.

Reach out to the sick

We are to continue the healing ministry of Jesus. World Day of the Sick is a good time to talk about this. Ask children how they feel when they are sick. Having empathy for other people is an important quality to work on with children. Talk also about ways to reach out to people who are sick or injured.

Ways to help the sick or injured

- Call a friend who is sick.
- Create a colorful get-well card.
- Say, "I hope you feel better soon."
- Visit someone with an injury.
- Be quiet, not loud, when you're with a sick person.
- Pray for people who are sick.

Encourage children to suggest other ideas for helping sick people. Children learn from one another. Remind children to pray for people who are caregivers to the sick as well.

Saints who helped lepers

World Day of the Sick is an opportunity to share the example of saints who helped sick people. Tell children about St. Damien de Veuster. He went to help people with leprosy who were sent away and could never go home again. At the leper colony in Molokai,

Hawaii, people lived in terrible conditions. St. Damien celebrated Mass, built houses and a church, and even dug graves for the dead.

Share also about St. Marianne Cope, who went to Molokai to help the people who had leprosy. She stayed to carry on the work of St. Damien after he died. She worked every day to make life better for the people. St. Marianne also cared for children who became orphans when their parents died of leprosy.

Open our hearts

Remind children that we are called to help sick people like Jesus did. Provide an opportunity for children to reach out to children in the local children's hospital. Collect arts and craft supplies for children to use. This is a great project for all ages for World Day of the Sick.

Give children and families a list of needed items, including washable paints, brushes, paint pens, watercolors, painting paper, jewelry-making kits, colored paper, scissors, and glue sticks. Let your learners know that this project makes the days a little brighter for sick children and gives them something to do. Deliver the items to the hospital for the Child Life team to distribute.

Pray for the sick

Jesus, healer of the sick,
on World Day of the Sick,
we remember those who are sick
at home, in the hospital, or in care centers.
Help people who are sick or injured
to know that you are always with them.
May we speak words of comfort and hope
in your name to people who are sick. Amen.

Ash Wednesday

We begin the season of Lent on this special day. Beginning with Ash Wednesday, we walk through the forty days of the lenten season. We use this time to renew our hearts and our lives. During Lent, we let God work in us. Lent should make a difference in how we live during the rest of the year. We turn away from whatever keeps us from God and turn toward the light of the resurrection of Jesus at Easter.

Ash Wednesday crosses

Ash Wednesday is the beginning of the season of Lent. Explain to children that during Lent we walk with Jesus. Lent reminds us to put Jesus first in our hearts and our lives. Each Lent can be a time of new beginnings on our faith journey.

Share with children that on Ash Wednesday, we can be signed with the cross on our foreheads as a reminder to always follow Jesus. As we walk the forty days of the season of Lent, we walk toward Easter and the new life that Jesus Christ brings to all of us.

Living Lent

The season of Lent is a time to let go of what keeps us from following Jesus. Explain to children that the changes we make during Lent can be the beginning of a deeper relationship with our Lord. During Lent, we focus on walking with Jesus each day.

Ask children to think of ways to follow Jesus on Ash Wednesday and through the season of Lent. This helps them work toward being all that God created them to be.

Ideas for living Lent

- Forgive a person who hurt your feelings.
- Say something nice instead of complaining.
- Share what you have with those who have less.
- Learn a new prayer by heart and pray it each day.
- Pray each morning and offer the day to God.
- Help someone with chores.
- Give thanks to God for loving you.
- Pray for a person who is having a tough day.
- Tell someone that Jesus loves them.
- Choose to follow Jesus even when it is hard.

Children learn from other children, and learning is multiplied. Help children understand that we are to live Lent. Suggest that children share their ideas with their families.

Pray during Lent

Ash Wednesday is a good time to talk to children about the three themes for Lent. The first theme is prayer. Stress that prayer is an important part of our relationship with God. Explain that there are many ways to pray to our God.

WAYS TO PRAY DURING LENT
Pray a prayer to thank God for the good things in your life.
Pray in your own words and ask God to help you.
Pray for the needs of other people in our world.

Ask children to name other ways to pray. Remind them that they can pray in many ways. Stress that God is always with us and hears our prayers.

Fast during Lent

The second theme of Lent is fasting. Explain to children that many people think fasting is only doing without food. But we can fast in other ways too. We can make small changes to be more like Jesus.

WAYS TO FAST DURING LENT
Fast from arguing and say something positive.
Fast from anger and ask for help with a problem.
Fast from uncertainty and trust in God.

It is not enough just to give up something: we must replace it with something positive. For example, if we fast from food, we give the money saved to a charity.

Give during Lent

Tell young people that the third theme of Lent is giving. We can give time, attention, and caring to others, as Jesus did. During Lent, we open our hearts and our lives to other people. We can make a difference.

WAYS TO GIVE
Share a talent, such as music, with the elderly.
Take time to talk to someone who seems sad or lonely.
Help with your parish food drive.

Jesus sends us to help others. Explain that we are to share what we have with those who have less. In this way, we walk with Jesus during Lent and beyond.

Service during Lent

During Lent, we get ready to celebrate the joy of Easter with others. A great service project for Lent for all ages is to collect items for Easter bags to be given to children living at a family shelter. By doing this during Lent, the Easter bags can be delivered to the shelter in time for children to have them on Easter morning.

Tell children that good items to collect for the bags include jump ropes, bubbles, toy cars, sidewalk chalk, and one-person games. After items are collected, older children can help fill colorful Easter bags with donated items. Be sure they select a variety of toys to put in each Easter bag.

Pray to live Lent

Lord Jesus Christ,
we ask you to be with us on our journey
from Ash Wednesday through the forty days
of the season of Lent.
May we turn away from what keeps us from you
and turn toward your light and your love.
Help us to follow your way
during Lent and always. Amen.

Feast of the Annunciation

On March 25, we remember how Mary said yes to God's plan for her life. She would be the mother of Jesus. Mary trusted in God. We are called to say yes to God in our lives like Mary did. We celebrate the feast of the Annunciation to honor Mary as the mother of Jesus. She is an example for all of us. She was faithful to God in all things, even when life was difficult. We can remember her example when we experience difficulties in our lives. We can ask Mary to pray for us to her Son, Jesus.

Mary said yes

The story of the Annunciation is found in Luke 1:26–38. Read it to the children. Share that on the feast of the Annunciation, we celebrate how Mary said yes to God's plan that she would be the mother of Jesus. Use questions to help children understand the gospel story.

Questions about the Annunciation

Where did God send the angel? *(Nazareth)*

What was the angel's name? *(Gabriel)*

Who did the angel go to? *(Mary)*

Who was Mary engaged to marry? *(Joseph)*

What did the angel say to Mary?
(She would be the mother of Jesus)

Who was Mary's cousin? *(Elizabeth)*

What did the angel say about her? *(She would have a baby too)*

What did Mary say to the angel? *(yes)*

What should we say to God? *(yes)*

Ask children if they have any questions. This provides an opportunity for children to learn and understand.

Hail Mary prayer

We honor Mary as the mother of Jesus and our mother. She was faithful to God in all things. Let children know that we can ask Mary to pray for us to her Son, Jesus. A favorite prayer to Mary is the Hail Mary. Make a copy of this prayer for each child. Then talk about it with your group of children. Explain to children that the Hail Mary has two parts.

In the first part of the Hail Mary, we honor Mary. These words come from the gospel where Gabriel visits Mary: "And coming to her, he said, 'Hail, favored one! The Lord is with you'" (Luke 1:28). We hear this gospel on the feast of the Annunciation.

The second part of this prayer is from the gospel where Mary goes to visit her cousin. Elizabeth says to her, "Most blessed are you among women, and blessed is the fruit of your womb" (Luke 1:41–42).

After talking about the prayer, pray the Hail Mary together. Encourage the children to pray this prayer at home too.

Say yes to God

On the feast of the Annunciation, we hear the story of God sending an angel to Mary. This gospel speaks to our lives too. Explain to children that we are to say yes to God in our lives, just as Mary did. She is an example of faith for us. Talk about ways we can say yes to God in our lives.

Explain that each day we are to say yes to the God who created us and who loves us without end. We need to be aware of God at work in our lives and become the people God created us to be. We do not do this alone, for God is with us always.

Say yes to God

- Yes, I will trust always in God.
- Yes, I will help other people.
- Yes, I will be a person of prayer.
- Yes, I will let God work in me.
- Yes, I will be a peacemaker.
- Yes, I will live God's purpose for my life.
- Yes, I will share the good news.
- Yes, I will serve others in God's name.

Small-group sharing

Look at some Bible stories about Mary with children. Point out that Mary is an example of faith in God for all of us. One activity for the feast of the Annunciation that helps children to learn about Mary is using small groups. Ask each group to look up a different Bible story and then tell the group about it. Here is a list of some of the Bible stories about Mary.

Bible stories about Mary

The Annunciation (LUKE 1:26-38)

Mary visits Elizabeth (LUKE 1:39-45)

Mary praises God (LUKE 1:46-49)

The birth of Jesus (LUKE 2:1-20)

Finding Jesus in the temple (LUKE 2:41-52)

The wedding at Cana (JOHN 2:1-11)

Mary at the cross (JOHN 19:25-27)

Mary in the upper room (ACTS 1:13-14)

The first disciple

Explore with your young people how Mary is the first disciple of Jesus. At the Annunciation, she agrees to be the mother of Jesus. She shares the good news of Jesus with her cousin Elizabeth. Mary stays close to Jesus during his life and at his death. After Jesus dies, she is in the upper room praying with the other disciples when the Holy Spirit comes to all of them.

Jesus calls us to be his disciples too. Share with your learners that there is no age limit on being a disciple. No one is too young or too old. Right now, right where we are, we are to witness to what Jesus Christ said and did. We are to trust in God as Mary did.

Children learn from one another in this way. Send home the list of Bible stories about Mary so families can continue the learning at home.

Pray to trust in God

Mary, mother of Jesus,
as we celebrate the feast of the Annunciation,
we remember that you said yes
when God asked you to be the mother of Jesus.
We honor you today for your trust in God.
Pray for us to say yes in our lives
to what God asks of us. Amen.

Triduum

THE HOLIEST TIME OF THE CHURCH YEAR IS THE TRIDUUM (A LATIN WORD THAT MEANS "THREE DAYS"). This season of the church year begins when Lent ends on Holy Thursday. This three-day season is from sunset on Holy Thursday to sunset on Easter Sunday. During the Triduum, we celebrate Holy Thursday, Good Friday, and Easter, including the Easter Vigil and the Mass of the Resurrection of the Lord on Easter Sunday. When the Triduum ends on the evening of Easter Sunday, the fifty-day Easter season begins.

A three-day season

The Triduum is a season of the church year between Lent and Easter. Explore this season with the children in your group. We celebrate Holy Thursday, walk through Good Friday, and then share the joy of the Easter Vigil and the Mass of the Resurrection on Easter. Share with children that the Triduum is the high point of the church year.

During the Triduum, we honor Jesus Christ, who came as the Savior for all people. Remind children that Jesus brought new life to us through his life, death, and resurrection. Help children walk through the days of the Triduum together so they begin to understand what we celebrate together as a church.

Holy Thursday

We begin the Triduum with the Mass of the Lord's Supper. Jesus gave us the Eucharist so he would always be with us in a special way. What an amazing gift Jesus has given us! We celebrate the Eucharist at each Mass and go out to serve others in his name.

Serve others for Jesus

On Holy Thursday night, Jesus told his disciples, "I give you a new commandment: love one another" (John 13:34). Talk with children about serving others as Jesus did.

Ways to show care to other people

- Do something nice without being asked.
- Spend time with someone who is lonely.
- Help another student with homework.
- Listen when someone wants to talk.
- Give to Operation Rice Bowl.
- Say thank you to someone who helps you.
- Compliment someone on a project.
- Be kind to a new child at school.

Let young people contribute their own ideas too. Be sure children listen with respect to the ideas of others. We are all on this faith journey through the Triduum together.

Pray on Holy Thursday

Lord Jesus Christ,
as we walk through the Triduum, we remember
that, at the Last Supper, you gave us the gift
of your presence in the bread and wine.
On this blessed Holy Thursday, we give you thanks.
Strengthened by the Eucharist, help us to serve others
and live as your disciples each day. Amen.

Good Friday

As we continue our walk through the Triduum, we remember that Good Friday is called "good" because we know the rest of the story. Emphasize to your learners that after Jesus died, he rose from the dead and brought new life to all of us. Every time we see a cross, we remember how much Jesus loves us. We look forward to celebrating the joy of the resurrection on Easter.

Make sticker crosses

Explain to children that there is no Mass on Good Friday. On this day, we hear the story of the passion, death, and burial of Jesus from the Gospel of John. We walk with Jesus to the cross and beyond. The last words of Jesus on the cross are "It is finished" (John 19:30).

Guide children to make simple crosses as a reminder of Jesus. They cut out five-inch cross shapes from colorful card stock, such as yellow, blue, purple, and green. Then they put a large cross sticker in the middle. These stickers are sold by the roll and are easy for even young children to handle. Encourage them to make more than one cross and give the others away. We remember that Jesus redeemed us and brought us new life.

Pray for Good Friday

**Jesus, Savior of the world,
we thank you for all that you have done
out of your unending love for each of us.
May we remember that you died on a cross
on Good Friday so we might have
the new life of Easter. Amen.**

Easter Vigil

The Easter Vigil is held on the Saturday night before Easter. We celebrate the journey of Jesus from death on a cross to the light of the resurrection. There are four parts to the Mass at the Easter Vigil: Service of Light, Liturgy of the Word, Liturgy of Baptism, and Liturgy of the Eucharist. The Triduum continues through Easter Sunday as we celebrate the new life Jesus brings to us by his life, death, and resurrection.

Easter egg table decorations

Show children how to make colorful Easter table decorations for a care center in your community. Get large Easter egg shapes precut from craft foam in a variety of colors. Also get packages of spring-themed foam stickers, such as flowers and butterflies.

Encourage children to share the hope of Easter time with elderly people. Show children how to decorate large foam Easter egg cutouts with spring-themed stickers. Each child will need to make several egg decorations to have one for each resident's place at mealtime. The decorations look great on the tables.

After dinner on Easter, each resident takes his or her Easter decoration to display in their room. In this way we share the hope of Easter with elderly people in the community.

Prayer for the Triduum

**God of hope,
we praise you for your love for us
and for sending Jesus as a Savior for all people.
As we celebrate the Triduum, help us to remember
that we walk with Jesus from darkness to light.
Help us to live as resurrection people
and share the hope of Easter with others. Amen.**

Easter Sunday

WE CELEBRATE THE MASS OF THE RESURRECTION OF THE LORD ON EASTER SUNDAY, WHICH CAN FALL IN MARCH OR APRIL. This is the most important day of the church year. We rejoice and remember all that our God has done for us. We know that Jesus Christ has risen and brought new life to all of us. The Easter season is a time of hope and joy that lasts for fifty days. Alleluia!

The Easter story

The story of the resurrection of Jesus on Easter reminds us that Jesus came for all people. Explain to young people that the four gospels tell how the women found the tomb empty on Easter morning. They went to tell the disciples, who then went to the empty tomb. Share an Easter gospel story with children, such as Matthew 28:1–10, Mark 16:1–8, Luke 24:1–12, or John 20:1–20.

Invite the children to ask questions. Explain that it was not until people actually saw the risen Christ in their lives that they really understood the significance of the empty tomb. We know what the empty tomb means because we know Jesus is risen. Alleluia!

Sprinkling rite

The celebration of Easter goes on for fifty days. At Sunday Mass during the Easter season, there is often a sprinkling rite with holy water. The water is blessed and sprinkled on the people at Mass. This is a reminder of our baptism and our new life in Jesus Christ.

Explain to children that as the priest sprinkles us with holy water during the sprinkling rite, we make the sign of the cross. This was done on our foreheads at baptism. Now we make the sign of the cross ourselves as a sign of our faith in our God who is Father, Son, and Holy Spirit.

Share Easter hope

Easter is a season of hope. Emphasize to children that we are to live in hope and to share that hope with others.

Ways to live in hope

- Praise God for the new life of spring.
- Remember that Jesus came for each of us.
- Sing out "Alleluia!" to God at Mass.
- Know in your heart that God loves you.
- Thank someone who has been kind to you.
- Celebrate that God is always with us.

Show children that our lives are full of hope because of Jesus. When they know that God loves them, they have hope, and that is a gift for a lifetime.

Praise God

Tell children that one of the psalms that we sing at Mass during the Easter season is Psalm 100. This beautiful psalm helps us give praise to our God together. Say each line and do the gestures. Children echo what the catechist says and does line by line.

Psalm 100 echo pantomime

Sing joyfully to the Lord!	*hands by mouth*
Serve the Lord with gladness,	*arms outstretched*
and come before him with joyful song.	*hands by mouth*
Know that the Lord is God:	*nod head yes*
he made us, we belong to him,	*hands over heart*
we are his people, the flock he tends.	*arms outstretched*
Give thanks to him, bless his name.	*fold hand in prayer*
The Lord is good,	*hands on heart*
his mercy endures forever.	*arms wide*

Be Easter people

We are Easter people because of the resurrection of Jesus. Share with children that we are to be Easter people during the season of Easter and in our lives each day. We celebrate the Easter season and the new life that Jesus Christ brings us.

Live as Easter people

- Give praise to God.
- Tell others about Jesus.
- Do acts of kindness.
- Trust in God always.
- Respect people of all cultures.
- Share hope with other people.
- Comfort someone who is sad.
- Look for the good in others.
- Welcome new children.
- Pray for the needs of others.

We know that Jesus has risen and we have new life through him. Jesus came for each one of us. At Easter, we rejoice in just how much God loves us.

Butterfly wreath

We are filled with joy at Easter because of our new life with Jesus due to his life, death, and resurrection. We remember all that Jesus has done for us and that Jesus came for all people. Encourage children to share the hope of Easter with others. They can make a butterfly wreath and give it away. Butterflies are a reminder of the new life Jesus brings to us at Easter.

Show children how to cut out a paper wreath from green card stock. Then each child decorates their individual wreath with colorful butterfly stickers. Encourage children to give their wreath to someone special. Talk about who this might be, such as a grandparent, a teacher, or a family friend. Butterfly wreaths remind us of the resurrection of Jesus and the new life he brings to all of us.

An example of faith in God

Share the story of St. Augustine with the children. This saint lived a long time ago, but his life and example of faith still teach us about following Jesus. Augustine's mother, St. Monica, prayed for a long time for his conversion. He finally turned away from sin and toward the light of Christ in his life.

His faith in God and his writings still provide inspiration today. Share that St. Augustine said, "We are an Easter people and alleluia is our song." Remind children that these words remind us to celebrate each day of the Easter season and beyond. We are Easter people.

Pray to live as Easter people

God of blessings,
as we celebrate the fifty days of Easter,
we praise you and rejoice in all
that you have done for us.
You sent Jesus Christ to bring new life
to people of all generations.
Help us to live always as Easter people
and give glory to your name. Alleluia.

Earth Day

PEOPLE ALL OVER THE WORLD OBSERVE THIS SPECIAL DAY ON APRIL 22 EACH YEAR. On Earth Day, we focus on protecting the earth and its resources for all people. Our planet is filled with wonders, and we must keep it that way. God created the resources of our earth for all people to share. As Catholics, we can join our efforts in celebrating Earth Day with others. We give thanks to God for the amazing gifts in our world. We show our gratitude by working to take care of what our God has given us.

Our amazing world

Our planet is an amazing home that God made for us. The variety of animals, mountains, waterfalls, rain forests, coral reefs, and people remind us that our God is an awesome God. Share with children that each of us can make a difference. We are called to care for the world and the people around us.

On Earth Day, show a video featuring some of the earth's wonders, such as *Planet Earth*, the award-winning series from the BBC, or whatever is available through your library. *Planet Earth* shows children of all ages places in creation that they might not know even existed. Encourage children to share what they liked best in the video. Remind them to give thanks to God. It was God who created us, our world, and everything in it.

Work together

Pope Francis, in *Laudato Si': On Care for Our Common Home* (vatican.va), reminds us that "the climate is a common good, belonging to all and meant for all." Talk with children about what this means. We should work together to protect the environment for all people.

We are seeing the effects of climate change around the world with extreme heat and flooding. Stress that God created our world for all people, and all of us are to care for our planet. An excellent guide to *Laudato Si'* is available on the United States Catholic Bishops' website (usccb.org). It includes activities, questions, prayers, and more that can be used for Earth Day. This special day for all people is one that Catholic kids should celebrate too.

Earth Day posters

God made a beautiful earth for us to enjoy. Stress to children that creation is a gift from God given out of love for us. We must work together as God's people to care for the earth so all people will have what they need. Ask young people to brainstorm ways to make a difference.

Ways to help our earth

- Recycle plastic, paper, and cardboard.
- Walk more places.
- Use less water.
- Eat locally grown foods or plant a vegetable garden.
- Reuse containers.
- Learn about solar power.

Then divide children into small groups of three. Give out poster board and markers to make Earth Day posters. Ask each group to make a poster showing a way to help take care of the earth's resources. When children have finished, ask each group to show their poster to the class and tell about it. This multiplies learning.

A saint who praised God

Share with your learners that St. Kateri Tekakwitha loved all of God's creation. As a member of a Native American tribe, she lived in what is now upstate New York. She endured many hardships, including smallpox and the deaths of her parents.

Tell children that as a young woman, Kateri learned about Jesus and was baptized by Jesuit missionaries who came to her village. She loved God with all her heart. When she went into the forest to gather wood for fires, she gave praise to God for the beauty of the world around her.

People in her village turned against her because of her baptism. She later had to flee to a mission 200 miles away. There she helped children learn about God. Share with children that she is a patron saint of ecology and the environment, which makes her story a good one for Earth Day. Remind children to give praise to God for creation like St. Kateri did.

Prayer circle

Before gathering with children, think of various things for which they are thankful to God. Write out creation prayer cards on brightly colored index cards. Make enough so each child is able to participate in leading part of the prayer. This is a good way to involve all children in a praise prayer for Earth Day.

Creation prayer cards

For the sun, moon, and stars
For mountains and rain forests
For rivers and oceans filled with life
For families and friends
For dolphins, seals, and penguins
For elephants and animals in the jungle
For lakes and waterfalls
For trees and flowers
For music and laughter
For giving us life
For people of all nations
For God's love for each of us

When you gather with the children, ask each child to choose one of the cards from a basket. Gather in a circle for prayer. One at a time, each child reads what is on his or her card, and all children respond, "Thank you, God." This prayer activity reminds children of some of the amazing gifts our God has given us.

Pray to care for our world

God of all creation,
thank you for making a wonderful world
for us to live in and share with others.
We know that everything you made is good
and created out of your love for all people.
Help us to take good care of the earth
on Earth Day and every day
and to encourage others to do this too. Amen.

Pentecost Sunday

JESUS PROMISED TO SEND THE HOLY SPIRIT TO THE DISCIPLES, AND THIS SPECIAL DAY FULFILLS THAT PROMISE. On Pentecost Sunday, we celebrate how the Holy Spirit came to the disciples and to Mary. The Holy Spirit guides our lives and our church from generation to generation. We remember that our God is Father, Son, and Holy Spirit every time we make the sign of the cross. The Holy Spirit guides our hearts and our lives as disciples of Jesus Christ.

The coming of the Holy Spirit

The feast of Pentecost is celebrated fifty days after Easter. Emphasize to children that this is the birthday of the church. Tell children that on Pentecost, the Holy Spirit came to the disciples and Mary in the upper room where they had gathered.

Read to children the story of the coming of the Holy Spirit in Acts 2:1–4. Stress to them that the Holy Spirit comes to us also. We pray to the Holy Spirit to guide our hearts and our lives and our church.

Share the good news

As Pentecost people, we are to share the good news of Jesus Christ with others, as the disciples did. Remind your young people that Jesus came for all people and all nations.

Explain to your group that we are to live what we believe. The Holy Spirit helps us share the good news of Jesus with others.

Ways to tell others the good news of Jesus

- Invite someone to go to Mass with you.
- Reach out to people in need.
- Tell people that Jesus loves them.
- Love others in the name of Jesus.
- Pray for the needs of other people.

Diversity enriches us

After the Holy Spirit came to the disciples on Pentecost, they went to share the good news of Jesus Christ with people from many places. Explain to children that the people heard the good news in their own language through the work of the Holy Spirit.

Stress that Pentecost shows us that the church is for all people. The diversity of the church, made up of people of many cultures, enriches the lives of all of us.

How to live in a global world

- Show respect to people of all cultures, skin colors, and religions.
- Welcome people of other cultures to Mass.
- Include a variety of children as your friends.
- Learn about different cultures and traditions.
- Get to know a new student who is different from you.
- Remember that Jesus came for all people and all nations.

Remind children that diversity has been part of the church since the beginning, at Pentecost. Encourage them to accept all people as God created them. We should do this not just on Pentecost, but all through the year. We remember that Jesus came for all people.

Holy Spirit prayer cards

Encourage children to pray to the Holy Spirit at Pentecost and beyond. Explore the idea that prayers do not have to be long. We can pray short prayers too. This helps children make prayer to the Holy Spirit part of their everyday lives.

Prayers to the Holy Spirit

Come, Holy Spirit,
show me the way to follow Jesus
in my life today and always. Amen.

Come, Holy Spirit,
fill my heart with your love
and help me see Jesus in others. Amen.

Come, Holy Spirit,
guide me to live the purpose
for which God created me. Amen.

Come, Holy Spirit,
give me the strength
to face challenges in my life. Amen.

Come, Holy Spirit,
open my heart and my life
to the needs of other people. Amen.

Come, Holy Spirit,
help me make a difference today
in the life of at least one person. Amen.

To make Holy Spirit prayer cards, print prayers on a variety of colors of card stock. Six prayers will fit on each sheet. Cut them apart and put them in a basket. Invite children to take home one or more prayers.

Open our hearts

Pope Francis told us, "Let yourself be renewed by the Spirit." Stress to children that we must open our hearts to let the Holy Spirit work in our lives.

Live Spirit-filled lives

- Pray to the Holy Spirit.
- Have compassion for others.
- Go to Sunday Mass each week.
- Listen to what people you trust say.
- Help people in need.
- Talk to a child who seems sad.
- Forgive someone who hurt your feelings.
- Treat all people with respect.

Ask children to think of other ideas too. We pray to the Holy Spirit to show us the way to live the life for which we were created.

Pray at Pentecost

Holy Spirit,
Come into our hearts and our lives
as we celebrate the great feast of Pentecost
and the birthday of our church.
Give us the courage to live in faith, hope, and love.
Show us how to be a community of God's people
and walk as disciples of Jesus Christ
now and always. Amen.

Mary, Mother of the Church

Pope Francis declared that the Monday after Pentecost is a day to honor Mary as the mother of the church. This title for Mary is not new, but the worldwide feast day is new. This special day honors Mary and celebrates her role in our church and in our lives. We ask Mary to pray for us to her Son, Jesus. We know that Jesus will hear her prayers.

Feast-day gospel

Explain to children that there is a new feast day celebrated around the world. It honors Mary as the mother of the church. Share that the gospel reading for this day is from John 19:25–31. The gospel story tells us that Mary and John were at the cross when Jesus was dying. They stayed even when other disciples ran away. Explain that from the cross, Jesus said to his mother, "Woman, behold, your son" (verse 26). He then asked John to care for Mary, saying, "Behold, your mother" (verse 27).

Mary at Pentecost

Mary was also present at the birthday of the church on Pentecost. In Acts 1, we hear how the eleven disciples were gathered in Jerusalem along with Mary, the mother of Jesus. They prayed and then the eleven disciples chose Matthias to replace Judas.

In Acts 2, we hear how the Holy Spirit came like tongues of fire. Tell children how the Holy Spirit came to the disciples and Mary as they gathered in the upper room. Explain that the example of Mary shows us how to live with faith in Jesus at all times.

Pray a Mary litany

Explore with your learners that we honor Mary with many titles, including Mother of the Church. We can ask Mary to pray for us to her Son, Jesus, with a litany. Invite individual children to read a title for Mary. All respond with "pray for us" after each title.

Mary litany

Mary, morning star,	*pray for us.*
Mary, servant of God,	*pray for us.*
Mary, mother of our Savior,	*pray for us.*
Mary, undoer of knots,	*pray for us.*
Mary, queen of peace,	*pray for us.*
Mary, mother of hope,	*pray for us.*
Mary, first disciple of Jesus,	*pray for us.*
Mary, mother of the church,	*pray for us.*

Encourage children to pray to Mary at other times too. She is the mother of Jesus, the mother of all of us, and the mother of the church.

Some feast days of Mary

SEPTEMBER 8 ■ Birth of Mary
OCTOBER 7 ■ Our Lady of the Rosary
DECEMBER 12 ■ Our Lady of Guadalupe
JANUARY 1 ■ Mary, Mother of God
FEBRUARY 11 ■ Our Lady of Lourdes
MARCH 25 ■ Annunciation
MAY 13 ■ Our Lady of Fatima
AUGUST 15 ■ Assumption

Feast days of Mary

There are many other days to honor Mary besides this one. Each one is an opportunity to learn more about the example of Mary for our lives.

We follow the example of Mary and trust always in God's plan for our lives, as Mary did.

Give to Mary's Meals

This organization is named after Mary. It provides meals at school for children living in poverty in many areas of the world. Tell children that many children around the world are going hungry because crops have failed due to drought and families do not have money to buy food. More information is found at marysmeals.org.

Pray to God that we will take better care of our earth and that people will step forward to help those who are starving. May we join together to make a difference in the lives of others. It is up to each of us. Learning about Mary's Meals is a great activity for the feast of Mary, Mother of the Church. Encourage children to share with their families about this organization.

Pray to Mary, Mother of the Church

Mary, mother of the church,
we honor you as the mother of Jesus,
the mother of the church, and our mother too.
Pray for us to your Son, Jesus, that we may
love God and others in our lives, as you did in yours.
Pray also that we may trust always
in God's will as you showed us. Amen.

Feast of the Body and Blood of Christ

In the United States, we celebrate this feast day on the Sunday after Trinity Sunday. We remember the gift of Jesus in the Eucharist. The feast of the Body and Blood of Christ is also known as Corpus Christi, which is Latin for "Body of Christ." All over the world, people come together to celebrate this feast at Mass. We remember that receiving the Eucharist gives us strength for our life journey.

The Last Supper

Explain to children that on the feast of the Body and Blood of Christ and at each Mass, we celebrate the presence of Jesus in the Eucharist. At the Last Supper, Jesus celebrated the Eucharist with his disciples. He took bread and wine and turned them into his body and blood.

Share with children the story of the Last Supper: "While they were eating, [Jesus] took bread, said the blessing, broke it, and gave it to them, and said, 'Take it; this is my body.' Then he took a cup, gave thanks, and gave it to them, and they all drank from it. He said to them, 'This is my blood'" (Mark 14:22–23).

Stress that Jesus is truly present in the Eucharist in the form of bread and wine. In this way, Jesus is with us always. Receiving the body and blood of Jesus unites us with Jesus and with one another. Sharing the Eucharist is sharing in the life of Jesus Christ.

Gift of the Eucharist

Talk with children about the gift of the Eucharist that Jesus gives us and why we receive the Eucharist at Mass. The word "Eucharist" means "giving thanks." At the Last Supper, Jesus tells his disciples to continue to celebrate the Eucharist together in his name.

Why we receive the Eucharist

- Jesus told his apostles to do this in memory of him.
- The Eucharist helps us give thanks to God.
- The Eucharist unites us with God and one another.
- The Eucharist gives us hope in Jesus and hope in the future.
- Celebrating the Eucharist helps us live as disciples of Jesus.

What a wonderful gift Jesus has given us. Remind children to give thanks to God for the gift of the Eucharist not only on the feast of the Body and Blood of Christ but each time they go to Mass.

A saint who prayed

Share with your group the life of one of the saints who had a special devotion to Jesus in the Eucharist. This is a good way to show children how to put the feast of the Body and Blood of Christ into action. One saint with a devotion to Jesus in the Eucharist is St. Caterina Volpicelli, who prayed often in front of the Blessed Sacrament.

St. Caterina found that receiving the Eucharist was a blessing in her life. It gave her the strength to help people day after day. She was a person of compassion who reached out to homeless children and the sick. Her life and her love of the Eucharist witnessed to the love of Jesus for all people. We can remember her example on the feast of the Body and Blood of Christ.

Live as eucharistic people

The Second Vatican Council's Constitution on the Church said, "The Eucharist is the source and summit of the Christian life." Share this quote with older children on the feast of the Body and Blood of Christ. Explore the idea that not only are we to receive the body and blood of Jesus, but we are called to live as eucharistic people each day. We must love God and love others with all our hearts.

Be eucharistic people

- Follow Jesus in how we live each day.
- Be people of prayer.
- Reach out to people in need.
- Share the good news of Jesus.
- Live in peace with one another.
- Trust in God at all times.

Coming forward to receive Jesus in the Eucharist unites us not only with Jesus but with other people. Talk about ways to live as eucharistic people.

Ask children to think of other ways to live as eucharistic people. Jesus teaches us to live this sacrament in what we do each day. We are to share the love of Jesus with others.

Serve others

In the Eucharist, we are united with Jesus and others: as the *Catechism of the Catholic Church* says, "The Eucharist commits us to the poor" (#1397). Emphasize to children that when we come forward to receive the body and blood of Christ, we unite ourselves to Christ and to one another.

A service project helps young people celebrate the feast of the Body and Blood of Christ. Check with Catholic Charities for ideas to serve people in your community. Catholic Charities works across the United States with the elderly, the homeless, children, refugees, and others. They are always in need of items for various program. Look online at their wish list.

Welcome others

A great idea for the feast of the Body and Blood of Christ is to make it Welcome Sunday. As people of the Eucharist, we can make a special effort that day to welcome people at Mass who are new, who are visiting, or who we haven't met yet. At Mass, we celebrate the love of Jesus for all people. This is what it means to live in love as eucharistic people.

What can kids do? They can hold open the church doors as people come in. They can say hello to the person who sits next to their family. They can be patient as they walk behind someone with a walker. Invite children to share their ideas. Then challenge each child to do or say at least one thing to be welcoming on the feast of the Body and Blood of Christ. Let families know about the plan.

Pray to give thanks and praise

Lord Jesus Christ,
on the feast of the Body and Blood of Christ,
we thank you for the gift of the Eucharist.
We know that you are always with us
in this holy sacrament.
Help us to see you at work in our lives
and in other people.
May we live as eucharistic people
and give praise to you for this gift
in our lives each day. Amen.

World Day for Grandparents and the Elderly

THIS FEAST DAY IS HELD ON THE FOURTH SUNDAY OF JULY. POPE FRANCIS ESTABLISHED THIS SPECIAL DAY. He dedicated World Day for Grandparents and the Elderly to older people in our families, our community, and our world. We remember that Jesus came for all ages and all people. This special day is held worldwide. Pope Francis calls us to open our hearts to the needs of elderly people, especially those who are homebound or living in care centers. We must show compassion to the elderly.

The grandparents of Jesus

World Day of Grandparents and the Elderly is held near the feast day of St. Anne and St. Joachim, who are grandparents of Jesus. Explain that we celebrate these two married saints on July 26. Little is known about them since they lived a long time ago. Let children know that tradition says that Joachim was a shepherd. It is thought that Mary was born to them when they were older and that she was their only child.

St. Anne and St. Joachim must have been people of great faith in God to raise a daughter like Mary who trusted always in God.

Tell children that St. Anne and St. Joachim are the patron saints of grandparents. We ask them to pray for us to Jesus.

A saint who was kind to the elderly

The story of St. Jeanne Jugan can be shared with children in your group for the World Day of Grandparents and the Elderly. As a child, she lived in a one-room house with her family. Sometimes they did not have enough to eat. When she grew up, she became a nurse because she wanted to help people.

St. Jeanne took care of people who were elderly and poor and had nowhere to go. The work was not easy, but she did not complain. She treated the elderly with kindness. She urged others to do the same. Remind children that we are to help elderly people like St. Jeanne Jugan did and to treat them with kindness.

Help the elderly

Encourage children to reach out to elderly people on World Day of Grandparents and the Elderly. Talk about some ways to put into action the words of Pope Francis, who said, "Seek out those elderly persons who feel most alone, at home or in residences where they live. Let us make sure that no one feels alone on this day."

Ways to help the elderly

- Draw a picture for a grandparent.
- Speak with respect to older people.
- Open the door for a person with a walker.
- Go with your family to visit an elderly relative.
- Listen to a story an elderly person tells you.
- Pray for grandparents and the elderly.

Ask children to open their hearts to the needs of elderly people on World Day for Grandparents and the Elderly. Remind them to look for opportunities to be helpful to elderly people beyond this day too. Suggest that they ask their family for help with any project beyond their home.

Birthday gifts for seniors

Explain to your group that some elderly people have ongoing health problems and need help with meals. They are not well enough to go out for groceries or cook for themselves. Sometimes elderly people outlive their relatives and spend a lot of time alone. In many communities, volunteers for organizations such as Meals on Wheels deliver meals to elderly shut-ins to be sure they have food for at least one meal a day.

Some of these organizations try to give each person a small gift delivered with the meal on their birthday. Collect items for this project, such as body lotion, a magnifying glass, a pen and notepad, a small first aid kit, a flashlight, and a puzzle book. Ask children to imagine the smile on each person's face as they receive a gift on their birthday along with their meal. This is a great project to celebrate World Day of Grandparents and the Elderly.

Show respect to the elderly

Stress to young people that all of us should show respect to the elderly on World Day of Grandparents and the Elderly and at other times too. Older people have done much for the younger generations. They may have worked hard to be sure their families had what they needed. Many taught their children to love God and show compassion for people in need. They may have prayed for us and helped us in so many ways.

Now it is our turn. We should value the example of older people who tried to make the world a better place for all. Things may not always have turned out well for them, but they endured. Stress to children that we should show respect to elderly people and share God's love with them beyond just this day.

Pray for the elderly

Loving God,
we thank you for the wonderful gift
of grandparents and the elderly in our families,
our churches, our communities, and our world.
We pray that they will know
that you are always with them.
Show us how to reach out a helping hand
to those who struggle as they get older.
May we show our appreciation to elderly people
on World Day for Grandparents and the Elderly
and throughout the year. Amen.

The Assumption of Mary

WE CELEBRATE THIS FEAST DAY OF MARY ON AUGUST 15. The Assumption of Mary is celebrated around the world. The tradition that Mary was taken to heaven body and soul comes down through the ages to us from the first century. We honor Mary and her example of faith on this holy day each year. Mary has a special place in our church and in our lives. She is a model of trusting in God even in times of hardships. She loved God with all her heart and continues to intercede for us in heaven.

Mary visits her cousin

Let children know that on the feast of the Assumption of Mary, we celebrate that Mary went to heaven after her earthly life. This is a holy day of the church. We ask Mary in heaven to pray for us to her Son, Jesus.

The gospel on this feast day is Mary's visit to her cousin Elizabeth. Mary goes to tell Elizabeth the good news about Jesus. Read this story aloud to the children from Luke 1:39–45. Ask a few questions to be sure they understand the story:

Questions about the Visitation

Who did Mary go to visit? *(Elizabeth)*

Why did Mary do this? *(to tell her about Jesus)*

What did Elizabeth say to Mary? *(Blessed are you who believed)*

Where do we learn about this story? *(the Gospel of Luke)*

How can we be like Mary? *(tell others about Jesus)*

Mary prayer cards

Give children Hail Mary prayer cards to take home to remember the example of Mary. Creative Communications for the Parish has colorful prayer cards with the Hail Mary prayer on the back. Encourage children to learn this prayer by heart. These holy cards will help them remember to ask Mary to pray for us on the feast of the Assumption and beyond.

When children have something to take home, it reminds them that God is working in their lives outside the classroom. It helps make the connection that their relationship with God is for all times and places of their lives.

Mary praises God

Part of the gospel for the feast of the Assumption is Mary's prayer of praise to God. This prayer is called the Magnificat. This is a good gospel to share with children, especially Luke 1:46–49. This section includes these words: "And Mary said: 'My soul proclaims the greatness of the Lord; my spirit rejoices in God my savior. The Mighty One has done great things for me, and holy is his name.'"

The Magnificat is our prayer also. We can give thanks and praise to God for all that God has done in our lives.

Talk about the Magnificat of Mary

Why does Mary give praise to God?
(she is to be the mother of Jesus)

How does she praise God? *(with a prayer of praise)*

What are some of our blessings?
(God's love, caring people, creation)

How can we praise God like Mary?
(thank God, tell others about God)

Mary's Magnificat echo pantomime

Following is an adapted version of Mary's Magnificat with an echo pantomime story. It is based on Luke 1:46–55. Tell children that when Mary visits Elizabeth, Mary praises God for all that God has done for her. Say each line and do the gestures. Ask children to echo the words and gestures line by line.

Mary's Magnificat echo pantomime

And Mary said,	*hands by mouth*
"My soul proclaims	*stretch out arms*
the greatness of the Lord;	*arms lifted high*
and my spirit rejoices in God my savior.	*hands on heart*
For God has looked with favor on me.	*nod head*
God has done great things for me,	*arms lifted high*
and holy is God's name.	*bow head, hands folded*
God's mercy is for all generations.	*stretch out arms*
God has filled the hungry	*hands over middle*
and sent the rich away empty.	*push hands out*
God has helped Israel,	*nod head*
according to the promise God made."	*hands on heart*

Learning by doing with an echo pantomime helps children remember and understand a gospel story. Stress to children that, like Mary, we are to give thanks to God in our lives. God has given us life and many blessings. We should celebrate all that God has done for us, as Mary did in her Magnificat.

Sing a Mary song together

On the feast of the Assumption, sing or play a song such as "Hail Mary: Gentle Woman" by Carey Landry, from Oregon Catholic Press (ocp.org). Tell children that the words remind us that God chose Mary, and she is blessed among women.

This song, sung by various choirs, is found on YouTube. It is a calming, uplifting song to help us celebrate the Assumption of Mary. Music reaches children in a special way and speaks to their hearts. Music honors Mary on this feast day.

Pray to Mary

Mary, mother of mercy,
you are an example of faith for all of us
as we follow Jesus in our lives.
Pray for us, that we may always trust in God
in our lives as you did in yours.
We honor you on the feast of the Assumption
and ask you to pray to your Son, Jesus,
that we may be people of faith
in what we do each day.
In this way our lives give praise to God. Amen.